U0725534

从庭园到世博

——户田景观设计 30 年

Landscape Design of 30 Years

[日] 户田芳树　著

刘　佳　译

中国建筑工业出版社

图书在版编目(CIP)数据

从庭园到世博——户田景观设计 30 年／（日）户田芳树著；
刘佳译 . —北京：中国建筑工业出版社，2010.8
ISBN 978-7-112-12313-1

Ⅰ.①从…　Ⅱ.①户…②刘…　Ⅲ.①景观－园林设计－作
品集－日本－现代　Ⅳ.① TU986.2

中国版本图书馆CIP数据核字（2010）第153646号

责任编辑：戚琳琳
责任设计：陈　旭
责任校对：王　颖　姜小莲

从庭园到世博

——户田景观设计30年

[日] 户田芳树　著

刘　佳　译

*

中国建筑工业出版社出版、发行（北京西郊百万庄）

各地新华书店、建筑书店经销

北京嘉泰利德公司制版

北京方嘉彩色印刷有限责任公司印刷

*

开本：880×1230毫米　1/16　印张：12¾　字数：410千字

2011年2月第一版　2011年2月第一次印刷

定价：99.00元

ISBN 978-7-112-12313-1

（19587）

目录　Contents

卷首语 1　Foreword 1

能为业界前辈户田芳树先生的作品集作序，我深感荣幸。户田先生是当代日本著名的园林和景观设计师，他在日本以及近年来在中国的作品为很多设计师所喜爱，包括我本人在内。

我羡慕户田芳树先生的经历，包括他的日本传统园林的研习经历、在建筑设计师事务所工作的经历和遍访日本名园及广大的城市与乡村，以及他广泛的兴趣和爱好。这些个人经历是理解户田芳树先生作品的钥匙。

我深感户田先生是用心在设计，并为之所感动，这种感动不仅因为他的作品所体现的精到与高品质，更是因为其作品所体现的对土地的热情和对艺术的执着。户田先生精心呵护每个场地，小心翼翼地处理每个细部，并且不断反思自己的每个作品。这份热情是他不断创新和突破的源动力。

户田先生的作品是平易近人的。他从日本庭院中吸取营养，把园林作为生活的空间来设计。一切设计空间都是为人提供的舞台，人们可以在其中散步、闲坐、嬉戏、聊天……因此，户田先生关注人的使用与感受，关注近人尺度的细节处理，关注一棵树、一株草，这些大约比任何空洞的形式感都重要吧！

早在 2005 年日本爱知世博会上，我就曾造访过户田芳树先生的作品。作为世博会的景观总设计师，他为爱知世博园的巨大成功作出巨大贡献，特别他为该次世博"自然的睿智"主题的体现，有许多独具匠心的设计，至今给我许多美好的回味。

也许是缘分，当年我作为日本爱知世博会中国馆日的论坛主持人，曾面对来自中国各省市领导大加赞扬爱知世博会的环境和生态理念与成功的规划设计，其中包括对世博园景观设计中体现的生态和环境意识的赞美。几年之后，我与北大和土人设计团队有幸参与了 2010 上海世博会后滩公园的设计。读过户田先生的文字后，感同身受于设计期间的种种艰辛与喜悦。两者虽在设计形式上有许多不同，但有一点是共同的，那就是对人、对自然的关怀。

作为晚辈，我衷心祝贺户田先生在过去岁月里获得的巨大成功，同时期待先生今后能为日本、为中国、为世界奉献出更多精彩之作。

俞孔坚
北京大学建筑与景观设计学院　教授，院长
Turenscape 首席设计师

卷首语 2 Foreword 2

前些日子，户田先生来电话说是要在中国建筑工业出版社出版第二本作品集，希望我能为此书的出版写几句。这又让我回想起 2002 年出版户田芳树作品集的情景，并仔细阅读了当时为作品集写的序和后记。也许是有一段时间没有如此投入地写文章了，惊讶地发现当时写作时如此充满激情，以至于如今很难再写出那种文句，难怪总听人说，某某大师的作品还是初期的好！现在想想也许有道理。自感还未到达鼎盛期，却已叶落花凋。不过想想鲁迅先生的文章："家里院子种了两棵树，一棵是梅花，另一棵还是梅花……"。读起来似乎很有让人思考的余地。无论怎样，只能试着"再写几句"。

从 2002 年至 2009 年，已是有 7 年的工夫了，户田先生的作品又表现出怎样的风格变化呢？从作品内容上看似乎已不太强调对空间整体形态上的刻意追求，而更加注重对细部处理的描述。就好像看到一位不施胭脂的妇女，却比花枝招展的女郎更具内涵一样，作品更具欣赏性。那些表面上的装饰已不太重要，最关键的是追求内心的真实性，告诫人们关注不经意的发现，也许是石缝中的一棵小草、园路旁的一朵小花、草坪上的一对恋人、水岸边的一群儿童、林荫下的一块散石或是广场中的一片舞友。树丛中的芳香、枝杆上的蜻蜓、慢慢移动的蚯蚓、清脆的蟋蟀声……。在这里人们不需要任何的"形态"表示，而是静静地享受回味大自然的真谛。同时又赋予作品另一层面的表述，就好似忠告每一位采访者去进一步理解自然与人类的永恒关系。放弃自我，回归素朴，原真。寻求平凡中的不经意的发现……。也许这就是户田芳树先生的设计哲学，不知表达得是否准确，不过这是我从户田先生的作品中获得的真实感悟。

最后，衷心祝贺户田芳树先生第二本作品集在中国出版，同时也衷心祝愿，在不久的将来能看到第三本、第四本……作品集的相继出版。

章俊华
R-Land 北京源树景观规划设计事务所
2009 年 3 月

我与景观

户田芳树

1947年新生儿大潮之中，我来到了这个世上，出生在广岛县尾道市。当时每个家庭中都有同年龄人和多个兄弟姐妹，小镇中热闹非凡，四处散发着活力。我家位于平安时代建造的古刹——净土寺附近的南面坡地处，尾道河道和向岛造船厂美丽的风景就近在咫尺（图1）。

昭和27年（1952年），我还在上幼儿园的时候，小津安二郎导演的名作《东京故事》在我家附近拍外景。采景为期3天，就在我家。我还记得原节子、香川京子等著名演员，一边等着上镜，一边和年幼的我玩耍。虽然我家只是普通的住宅而非气派的旧宅，但是小津导演却发现在我家的院子里，可以清晰地看见净土寺里多宝塔的风景。当时我们全家并没有留意到这一点。虽然为仅仅只在电影中出现了很短的一段时间而感到沮丧，但电影中的场景却深深印记在我们的脑海里。从那以后，每年正月我们全家都会聚在一起，按照同样的角度取景、拍照（图2）。

上大学以后我开始学习景观学，学到了"风景只有被人意识到之后才能真正成为风景"的"发现风景"这一理论。小时候在家取景的电影正是如此，直到现在我仍然会想起这些。还记得，上高中时，我曾经和高中的朋友一起爬上后山，不厌其烦地看着眼下宽广的风景，在一起说了好多好多。现在想起来，两个光头的高中生就那么赞叹着"真是好风景啊"什么的，一起在后山待了那么久，真是一段令人发笑而又让人怀念的回忆（图3）。

多年以后，我设计了名为"Green Pier 津南"的雪原度假地。在漫天新雪、黑白两色的风景之中，高中时从后山上看到的尾道风景突然在眼前鲜明地浮现出来，可以说是一种不可思议的缘。那并非我刻意之作，而是不知不觉中造就了那样的形态（图4）。

要升大学的时候，我并不想学建筑，而是想学习能从稍广的角度进行把控的城市规划，或是要建造一种更加富有柔性的物体。那时我第一次接触到了"造园"这个词。向高中老师咨询后，也没有得到什么明确的指导，于是就抱着只能靠自己亲身体验才能明白的想法，上了东京农业大学造园系。

其实，我在大学里没有怎么好好地念过书。我参加了"管弦乐"和"日本庭院研究会"这两个社团，还在盆栽店里拼命打工。我从小学开始就喜欢古典音乐，要是到东

Landscape and I

By Yoshiki TODA

I was born in Onomichi in Hiroshima Prefecture in 1947, in the peak of post war baby boom years. There were many classmates and their brothers and sisters at practically every home in the neighborhood. The entire town was filled with liveliness. My father was an engineer of Manchuria Railway, and his heroic tale was having operated the steam locomotive of worldwide fame of then, Special Express Asia and had carried Imperial Prince Takamatsu. I remember begging him to tell me the story over and over again. Our house was situated on a south hillside adjacent to a historic temple, Jodo-ji that dates back to Heian period, and a clear panoramic view of the Onomichi Channel and the shipyard on the Mukojima Island（Fig.1）.

In 1952, when I was still in kindergarten, the movie director, Yasujiro Ozu's masterpiece, "Tokyo Story" was filmed in the neighborhood. For three days, the location team was in and out of our house, and I remember the actress like Setsuko Hara and Kyoko Kagawa waiting for their parts would play children's games with me. Our house was a small common house, not of an old family, but Ozu had discovered there was a great view of the pagoda of Jodo-ji through our yard. We ourselves had not paid notice of it until then, and although we were reluctant that in the movie it was a very short scene, the shot left an impression on me. Ever since then, it became a tradition to take a family picture on the new years day in the same angle as was in the movie（Fig.2）.

When I later studied landscape architecture in university, I learned that landscape becomes a landscape only when it is perceived in mind. I look back now that the experience was truly the "discovery of landscape." I also remember my high school days climbing up the hill behind our house with friends talking for hours enjoying the view of the landscape. I reminisce it as rather a humorous picture of cropped headed high school boys spending hours relishing the view（Fig.3）.

Some years later when I designed "Green Pier Tsunan," a winter resort in snow-covered region of Niigata Prefecture, I was amazed in wonders to find the unexpected view of Onomichi appearing in the monotone landscape of the first snowfall. It was indeed unintentional（Fig.4）.

At the time of applying for college, I had visions of taking up either urban planning, a field commanding larger scale than architecture, or in creating something softer. In pursuit of direction, I came across the word, "landscape architecture." I consulted my high school advisor but was not able to receive much enlightenment. I decided I would find out for myself, and chose to enter College of Landscape Architecture at Tokyo University of Agriculture.

Truthfully speaking, I was not a very diligent student in college. I joined the extra-curriculum activities of "orchestra" and "Japanese garden design study group" as well as spending much time moonlighting for a gardener. I had loved classical music since

1 故乡的风景 (View of my hometown)
2 全家福 (Picture of my family)
3 后山的风景 (View from the hill behind the house)
4 Green Pier 津南 (Green Pier Tsunan)
5 东福寺庭院，重森三玲作 (Tofuji Garden)
6 手琢氏庭院 (Mr. Teduka's House Garden)

京之后马上接触到音乐的话，说不定会在那条路上走下去。我还记得，当知道农大有"管弦乐"这个社团的时候，我还高兴得小跳了一会儿。不过我也不得不面对这样一个事实，这个管弦乐社团，从合唱部到器乐部竟然全都被别人瞧不起，我觉得自己必须为社团做些什么，于是那4年里，我真是拼了命地在努力。4年后，我们的社团成员超过了40人，也配齐了各种乐器，已经可以分两组来演奏贝多芬或是舒伯特的交响乐了。现在，是超过80人的大型管弦乐社团。

另一方面，"农大庭院研究会"加入了京都重森三玲氏流派，成为吉河功氏开办的"日本庭院研究会"旗下的一个组织。大一的夏天，重森氏带领我们参观了大德寺的瑞隆园和东福寺的方丈庭院，当时非常震惊（图5）。因为我有生以来还是第一次身处这样非凡的空间，它们根本就不是大学里学到的那些美丽的事物，而是凝聚了设计师的痛苦与喜悦的非凡空间。我想融入这个世界，哪怕只是那么一丁点也好，这种单纯的想法在心中油然而生。于是，我在东京的一个工头那儿接受锻炼，之后就去了京都。我清楚无知的可怕，心想去了京都之后应该可以从那遍地的高级庭院中学到不少东西。对于我这样一个从学生时代就看遍了全国各地的庭院，并在盆栽店磨炼过技术的人来说，京都这家普通的造园公司实在是很难让我发挥才干，那种地方充其量只是把技工召集在一起而已。不过那时，全国各地想学习庭院设计的人都聚集到了京都，晚上有学习会等活动，充满了活力。

离开京都之后，我回到故乡，在当地的一家造园公司工作了一段时间。非常幸运，当时竟然有人全权委托我负责建造一个庭院（图6）。我为此全力以赴。那是25岁的我倾尽所能建造的一个庭院，可惜只是一个重森三玲风格的虎头蛇尾之作。不过，当时的我为了能完成这一个庭院真的是竭尽了全力。不久，我辞去了那份工作，开始了一个人寻找造园工作的生活。那时我接到一份独自修整海边别墅庭院的工作，时间为一星期。除了海浪声、鸟鸣声和剪刀的咔嚓声还有母亲做的便当陪伴我以外，一整天没有任何人和我说一句话。就这样度过了一天又一天。偶尔想到自己可能还要干40年这样的活儿，就觉得前途简直是一片黑暗。

正好在那个时期，我从东京的同学那儿得到了一个消息，建筑家黑川纪章开办的城市设计（城市规划事务所）正在招募临时工。于是我筹措路费来到了东京，住进朋友家，并在事务所里实习了两个星期。我高中时曾经在杂志上看到过黑川先生的《HELIX CITY》，对他十分崇拜，觉得他

elementary school. Had I grown up in a city and been exposed to music much earlier, I would have pursued career in music. Therefore, I was thrilled to find there was an orchestra at Tokyo University of Agriculture. However, the reality of this orchestra was in a sorry state that it was being dismissed as "instruments" from the glee club. I took it upon myself to do something about it and literally sacrificed my four years at the university. By my senior year, there were over forty members with almost full range of instrumentation, became double winds and brass orchestra, and was able to perform Beethoven and Schubert symphonies. It has become today a large orchestra enjoying over eighty enlisted members.

Meanwhile, the No-dai Japanese Garden Research group was more or less a subdivision of Japanese Garden Research Association led by Mr. Isao Furukawa, who was one of the successors of Mirei Shigemori. Nevertheless, I was totally overwhelmed by the gardens of Daitoku-ji Zuiho-in and Tofuku-ji Hojo we visited in the summer of freshman year personally guided by Mr. Shigemori himself（Fig.5）. The gardens were far beyond the fixed studies at the college, but filled with mixture of agonies and joys of the creator, awesome space that I met for the first time in my life. Pure notion of wanting to come as close to this milieu grew in me then. In thus, after graduating and receiving a year of intensive training in Tokyo from a one-man gardener master, I moved onto Kyoto. I was innocently ignorant to believe that I would be able to learn top class garden design anywhere if it was in Kyoto. Having intensively traveled researching notable gardens throughout Japan in college as well as trained in gardening techniques, the landscape company I was hired was very disappointing. It was nothing but a group of labor hands. Nevertheless, there were many youths from all over the country who had come to Kyoto to study Japanese garden, evenings were spent actively with study groups.

Eventually, I resigned to return to my hometown and started to work for a local gardening company. Fortunately, in a soon time, one client gave me an opportunity to design and complete an entire garden. I was utterly excited. I tried to realize everything I had at the time I was age of twenty-five（Fig.6）. Nonetheless, the result was an immature imitation of Mirei Shigemori. It was the best I could deliver then. I left this company again after a while and lived on finding work here and there on my own. One time, I had about a weeklong commission to care alone a garden of a summer beach house. Bringing my mother's handmade lunch, day in and day out worked in solitary to the sounds of waves, birds and clipping of my shears. I was suddenly overcome by an anxiety my life was going to stay this way for next forty years.

It was in such days, I heard from a classmate in Tokyo that Kisho Kurokawa's urban development office was looking for part time hands. I managed to make some money to travel, and staying at friend's house, I experienced a two weeks work. I had seen Mr. Kurokawa's Project for Helix City featured in a magazine article when I was still in high school. I had thought he was one of the most brilliant architects and had aspiration for him ever since. I was able to join his company eventually and have had opportunities to discuss projects with him. He was as sharp as a knife and had an aura about him that is of

7 阿拉伯联合酋长国国际会议城模型 (Model of UAE Conference City)
8 山梨医科大学中庭 (Courtyard of Yamanashi Medical University)
9 山梨医科大学中庭 (Courtyard of Yamanashi Medical University)
10 Green Pier 津南 (Green Pier Tsunan)
11 Green Pier 津南 (Green Pier Tsunan)

比其他的建筑家帅多了。之后我成功地留在了事务所，并得到了和他探讨案例的机会。我感觉到他全身都充满着一种无所不能、凌驾于这个时代的自豪感。黑川先生的设计过程是这样的，首先让设计人员梳理条件，调查周边环境并陈述他们自己的意见。紧接着黑川氏就会提出他的"概念"和"内容"。然后设计人员需要为这些概念和内容准备理论依据。下一个阶段，由设计人员提出数个具有不同含义的方案。然后，黑川先生会当场画出草图。之后通过反复地研讨直至确定细节，逐步完成整个设计工作。

我仍然记得自己担任在迪拜的阿拉伯联合酋长国国际会场景观设计的那段日子。当设计工作开始停滞不前时，我询问黑川先生"该怎么办？"很意外，他竟然回答我说"景观设计这方面我不太懂。你先做几个方案给我看看。"几天后，我竟然从自己那些拙劣而幼稚的几个方案中获得了一个全新的想法，并构建出景观设计的大方向。我觉得这简直就像变魔术一样。之后我明白了，不应该让过往的经验使自己的设计思维趋向单一化，而是应该将多层次、多方面的放射性思维作为概念进行融汇与组合（见图7）。

1980年在我33岁的时候，几乎没有什么园林设计经验的我自立了门户。现在想来还真是够莽撞的。但是当时日本公共事业的发展正迎来最后的高潮期，只要肯拼，总是有活可干的。直到1990年为止，在创业初期的10年里做的那些重要项目，我觉得自己真是把从大学开始的这十几年所累积的能量一口气全都释放出来了。

第一份工作是设计"山梨医科大学中庭（1981年）"。因为是建筑的中庭，要求在设计时多采用建筑规划中常见的直线。但是我却认为可以融合用地外围景观，形成有机的设计，极力减少使用素材的种类，从而使其立显简洁才符合这个项目。从入口处眺望水面，庭院的背景为草坪堆坡，园内道路与河流均为曲线。从屋顶上拍摄的照片很好地展现了设计成果，整个中庭如同人体样貌一般。恰好中庭旁边的建筑物是解剖大楼，真可谓黑色幽默（图8、图9）。

在设计"Green Pier津南庭院（1985年）"的时候，我向设计大规模休闲娱乐空间的景观这一课题发起了挑战。这个4公顷的风景庭院，不仅引入周边雄伟的景色，还将山上的流水引入庭院内部，使其成为各种各样的瀑布、流水和水面，作为修景之用，由此营造了一个简洁、大气的空间。通过减少、压缩设计要素，凸显了自然风景的多样性。创造的景物为"地"，而背景为"图"，与传统意义上的"地"和"图"正好相互逆转，一种不可思议的风景油然而生（图10、图11）。在降雪量超过4m的地区，冬季看不清池塘的形状。新

a leader of his time. Project developing method in Kurokawa's office was, at first, staff assistants would organize the requisites, inspect the site area, and deliver their analysis. Kurokawa in no time will come up with a "concept" and a "program." Subsequently, the assistants will develop back up, and produce schematic plans with several different ideas. In response, Kurokawa will immediately right there and then elaborate the drawings. The meetings will be held successively through up into perfecting the details.

My unforgettable memory is when I was in charge of the landscape design project of UAE Conference City in Abu Dhabi. Along the work process, I had come to a deadlock and was lost. I consulted Kurokawa in what to do. To my dismay, he responded, "I do not know much about landscape design. You go ahead and bring me some drawings of your own ideas." When I later returned to him, over the few immature drawing plans of mine, he whipped up a completely new rendition and constructed the landscape directive. It was almost like magic. I understand now by experience that designing is not deliberated by building atop single directive, but by constricting a concept synthesized from ideas radiated from wide range of layers and directions（Fig.7）.

Without much experiences in landscape architecture, I established my own practice in 1980 at age of thirty-three. Now that I look back, it was reckless. Nevertheless, the public enterprise in Japan was evolving into final stage of its progress that there was work for us having made the effort. In a sense, the early major projects in the first decade up to 1990, was releasing accumulation of what I had acquired in the ten several years since graduating college.

My first project was the "Courtyard of Yamanashi Medical University"（1981）. As it was a space within architecture, application and intense usage reflecting the straight lines of the architecture was requested. However, I felt it was more appropriate to integrate outside landscape into organic but simple design with minimum selection of materials. From the entrance, water surface is viewed with a backdrop of gentle grass slope, and stream and walkway designed in curving lines. Photographed from the roof, intended effect is evident almost in the image of human body. As it so happened the adjacent building was the dissecting ward, it turned out to be something of a hidden black humor（Fig.8）（Fig.9）.

"Green Pier Tsunan Central Park"（1985）was a challenge of landscaping a large scale recreational park. A panoramic garden with site area of 4 ha constituted by incorporating the magnificent view of the area, utilizing water stream collected from the mountain into various elements as waterfall, stream, and a pond, simple yet dynamic space is achieved. By minimizing design elements, diversity of the natural landscape is enhanced making the designed objects the "ground" and the background the "figure, " a wondrous landscape of reversed "ground" and "figure" had emerged（Fig.10）（Fig.11）. This region where snowfall records over 4 meters, the outline of the pond disappears in the winter. The silhouetted landscape that appears for a very short moment with the first snowfall amazingly resembles that of my hometown, Onomichi. It could have been the memory of landscape that inhabits within me took control of my hands.

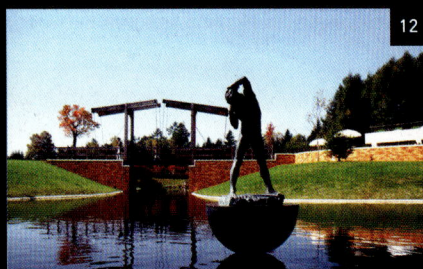

12 蓼科雕塑公园（Tateshina Sculpture Park）
13 蓼科雕塑公园（Tateshina Sculpture Park）
14 别府市政厅广场（Beppu City Hall Square）
15 别府市政厅广场（Beppu City Hall Square）
16 诹访湖畔公园（Suwa Lakeside Park）

雪时的风景竟然在一瞬间与我的故乡尾道的风景紧紧重叠在一起，这不可思议的景色令我感到震惊。也许正是那一直沉睡在我心中的故乡风景在推动着我的双手。

在下一份工作"蓼科雕塑公园（1989年）"的设计中，我也使用了同样的构思。规划阶段，把业主拥有的相当于真人大小的雕塑列为景观要素，构造了一笔成型的连续景观。雕塑的功能从单纯的供人欣赏转变为整体风景中的一部分，利用这块被森林和湖泊所包围的绝佳地点来开展景观设计。树林内斑驳的阳光配上与其相符的女性雕像，草地上能承受强烈蓼科（地名）日照的罗丹风格的男性雕像，充分体现了雕塑的质感（图12、图13）。

"别府市厅舍广场（1985年）"的小空间里，十分重视对水的形态设计。在确定两个最佳角度之后，开始了设计。从内侧弯曲的跌水中重复地落下的水与光交相辉映的场景，完全达到了预想的设计效果，结果令人满意。没想到从建筑物上方俯瞰广场时，规则、美妙的波纹竟然和铺装柔和的曲线完美地结合在一起，呈现了一幅出人意料的风景。并非刻意为之，而是顺其自然得到的意外之景，这也可称之为景观设计的一种深化（图14、图15）。

设计"诹访湖畔公园（1986年）"时，就民营企业在当地保持怎样的特性进行了认真的考虑。作为企业战略，世界第一的钟表制造商——诹访精工计划花费5亿日元建造一座公园，免费赠送给诹访市，通过这一活动，纪念成立25周年。精工选中了当时仅36岁年轻的我担纲景观设计。诹访湖作为一级河川，受到法律的严格保护，周边不可轻易进行开发，与法律有关硬性规定相抵触是这个项目中最大的难点。由于是民营企业出资建造，且诹访湖的情况比较特殊，国家和长野县政府对此都表示理解并给予支持，允许我们引入公园设施，使当时的难题得到了解决。位于公园中心诹访大社处的"御柱"，设计成摩登的"时间的象征"，面西而设，6月10日（精工成立纪念日）这天演现了太阳从柱间落下的风景，用夕阳表现了精工的历史（图16、图17）。

之后10年里，我经手的最重要的项目是"修善寺虹之乡（1990年）"。这个作品在1995年获得了日本景观界最高荣誉——日本造园学会奖。修善寺虽然是一个小镇，但政府机关的工作作风相当灵活，必要的时候择选必要人才，使得计划得以大胆地实施。一开始，我的工作是景观设计监修，之后，我又担任了总体工程设施、建筑、土木和景观的监修工作，并负责景观施工图设计。由于这是一个40公顷的大规模主题公园，在各领域相关专家的支持下完成

The next project, "Tateshina Sculpture Park" (1989) was also planned in the same philosophical approach. Bringing forth the client's life size sculpture statues as elements, the landscape was composed in a sequence that of a single brush stroke. The landscape design was developed emphasizing the superb location of surrounding woods and lake, diverting from art appreciation focus, the sculptures were integrated into the total landscape. Female statues were placed in the woods where the streams of sunlight through the leaves enhance the features the most, and Rodin like male statues out on the lawn where direct sunshine emphasizes the massive quality of the sculptures (Fig.12)(Fig.13).

At "Beppu City Hall Square" (1985) where space was limited, we focused on featuring the water composition. We began by determining two focal points. The effect of radiant sparkling of light against constant falling water from the inwardly arched cascade appeared as we had pre-calculated, and the outcome was rewarding. Furthermore, when observed from upper flowers of the building, there was a view of perfect ripple pattern steadily emerging on water surface corresponding the gentle curve of the pavement. It was unintentional wonders. It could be said by entrusting to nature, profoundness of landscape design will generate itself by interacting with non- anticipated phenomena (Fig.14)(Fig.15).

"Suwa Lakeside Park" (1986) was a project to think how a private industry should establish its identity in the local community. One of the leading watch manufacturers of the world, Suwa Seikosha Co., Ltd., upon its celebration of 25th year anniversary was to donate a park to the city of Suwa expending five hundred million yen. They had addressed for a younger landscape architect, and myself being thirty-six at the time was elected. Lake Suwa being a first-grade river, the obstacles were the laws and codes; however, as it was a private enterprise, national and Nagano Prefecture authorities did show understandings, and permitted the park to be realized otherwise impossible in those days. In the center was placed a designed monument, "Symbol of Time" representing the sacred pillars of Suwa Shrine. The monument was placed facing west in a position the sun will disappear in the horizon framed between the two pillars exactly on June 10th of each year commemorating Seikosha foundation day and "time memorial day." The history of Seikosha was expressed in the setting of sun (Fig.16)(Fig.17).

In the successive ten years, the most significant project was "Shuzenji Niji no Sato" (1990). The project was awarded in 1995, the most prestigious award in Japan from the Japanese Institute of Landscape Architecture. Shuzencho is a small town with its public office having unusual flexibilities. Electing necessary experts as necessitated, we were able to carry out the project quite daringly. Initially, my commission with the project was supervision for landscape design. However, eventually I undertook managing the entire enterprise; the facilities, architecture, engineering and landscape design as well as rendering of landscape architecture working drawings. As it was a large-scale theme park with 40 hectares of land, we managed to complete the project owing help from numerous experts in various fields.

17 诹访湖畔公园（Suwa Lakeside Park）
18 修善寺虹之乡（Shuzenji Niji-no-Sato）
19 修善寺虹之乡（Shuzenji Niji-no-Sato）
20 修善寺虹之乡（Shuzenji Niji-no-Sato）
21 三池韩国庭院（Mitsuike Korean Garden）

了汇总工作。

公园的游览路线利用自然地形建造而成，与公园的主题紧密相连，通过该路线在园内游览大约需要2～3小时。从英国购买的小型蒸汽火车，连接了英国村和加拿大村。利用山谷泄洪池建造了日本庭园，水池周围种植菖蒲、百合、石南等植物群，各个花季都吸引着前来参观的游客。手工艺区不仅有艺术家的工作室可供参观，还配备了互动参与系统。这种遵循自然地形、植栽天性来实现总体规划的体验，为我日后作为"爱·地球博（2005年）"景观总监的成功提供了很好的经验（图18、图19、图20）。

20世纪90年代，我接手了不少传统庭园的设计。我对韩式庭园一直很感兴趣，每年都去考察韩式庭园，还有幸参与了"三池韩国庭园（1994年）"的设计。这个庭园是神奈川县和京畿道友好城市关系的佐证。以李氏朝鲜时代文臣武将它邸为样本，整个庭园由前苑、前庭、主庭、后庭、后苑共5个空间构成，将韩国的家居生活和自然之间的关系所形成的风水思想作为设计的基础。我委托韩国的闵教授担任庭园的监修工作。约在1500年前，中国庭园文化经由朝鲜半岛流入日本。虽然在这段时期日本修建了各式各样的庭园，但日本独特的传统庭院还是有别于中国和韩国，逐渐地发展起来。为了追寻日本庭园设计的根源，我考察了韩国的庭园，却看到了与日本完全不同的韩式庭园风格，令我感受到根深蒂固的文化差异（图21、图22）。

另外有一次，对建于江户时代，位于日本东京东部、江户川区的"一之江名人老屋"进行考察、修复。住在东京的我，对身边能有历史如此悠久的出色建筑而感到惊讶（图23、图24）。

1990年我考察并修复了故乡尾道的净土寺。虽然这是江户时代末期（1860年左右）的庭园，却很难得地保留了当时的竣工平面图。我参考这张图纸，对寺庙进行了修复。约130年的时间里，树木一直在成长，使我切身感受到庭园会发生巨大变化的这一事实（图25）。

那段时期最热门的话题，是维也纳森柏龙宫殿内日式庭园的修复与再建工程。森柏龙宫殿拥有匹敌法国凡尔赛宫殿的巨大规模和华美造型，而其中的一角有座日式庭园。它是由宫廷园林设计师在1913年建造的，曾一度荒废，之后被修复。时隔85年，维也纳的市民终于得以再度观赏其中美景。至今市民们都将它视为珍宝（图26、图27）。

我从学生时代就开始孜孜不倦地学习日式庭园的设计，结果却在意想不到的地方发挥了作用。有许多日本景观设计师虽然一直关注传统的庭园和建筑，却因为得不到深入

If walked leisurely would take a good 2 to 3 hours, an excursion route conformed to natural geographical features was drawn connecting the attractions. Small steam locomotive was bought from England and installed to run between English and Canadian townscapes. Utilizing the reservoir in the basin, Japanese garden was created, and masses of irises, lilies and rhododendrons were planted for drawing seasonal visitors. In the handicraft zone, not only the visitors can observe the resident artists studios, but take part in creative activities. I doubt not my experience of coordinating the entire project, incorporating natural topography and following providence of vegetation, helped me later to achieve the result as the landscape director for the "Nature's Wisdom" Expo 2005 in Aichi (Fig.18) (Fig.19) (Fig.20).

In these years, there were number of commissions involving traditional gardens. "Mitsuike Korean Garden" (1994) was an opportunity I took part due to my long time interest in Korean gardens and annual survey trips. This garden was planned commemorating friendship between Kanagawa Prefecture and Gyeonggi Province. With residential estates from both the Liao and Joseon Dynasties as models, consisting of five sections, front garden, front court, main garden, rear court and rear garden, Korean residential space and natural landscape was realized respecting feng shui theories. Professor Min Kyung-Hyun from Korea had been invited as the advisor on garden design. Chinese garden culture was introduced to Japan through Korean peninsula approximately 1,500 years ago. Since then various gardens have been made; however, a very different style of gardens from either Chinese or Korean have developed. My research studies of Korean gardens were to determine roots of the Japanese, but I was to find total dissimilarity in its aspect. Cultural differences are much deeply rooted than I had imagined (Fig.21) (Fig.22).

There also was a survey and restoration project of an estate of Edo period in eastern district of Tokyo, "Ichinoe Nanushi Yashiki" (1998). It was a revelation to find such a historic and stately architecture still existed in the city (Fig.23) (Fig.24).

Another notable project was surveying and restoring the Jodo-ji temple in my hometown, Onomichi, in 1990. The garden was of late Edo period, circa 1860, but surprisingly there existed an as-built drawing of the time. The restoration work was carried out referencing the drawing. I was amazed at how in 130 years, with the trees grown taller, a garden would take on a drastic change in its appearance (Fig.25).

The most significant topic of the decade was the restoration and installation of the Japanese garden in the Schönbrunn Palace grounds in Vienna. The Schönbrunn Palace, with its beauty and scale matching that of the Versailles, was discovered having a Japanese garden in the grounds. It was built in 1913 by the palace gardener but had been ruined. It was restored after eighty-five years and opened to the public. It is being enjoyed and treasured by the citizens of Vienna (Fig.26) (Fig.27).

My extensive research studies in Japanese gardens since college was very much rewarded in these projects. It seems to me the Japanese landscape architects have interest and regard for traditional architecture and gardens, but not having had the opportunities

22 三池韩国庭院 (Mitsuike Korean Garden)
23 一之江名人古宅 (Ichinoe Nanushi Yashiki)
24 一之江名人古宅 (Ichinoe Nanushi Yashiki)
25 净土寺 (Jodo Temple)
26 维也纳森柏龙宫殿内的日式庭园 (Japanese Garden in the Schonbrunn Palace grounds in Vienna)

学习的机会而白白地错过时间，实在令人感到惋惜。我认为应该主动地创造深入学习的机会。

2000年之后大的项目要属2005年爱·地球博（爱知县），我接任了景观总监一职。从2001年年末开始，直到2005年9月30日会期结束，总共耗费了大约4年的时间。说实话，当时我根本不知道总监应发挥怎样的职能，应该怎么做才好，真的是在摸索中开始的工作。总监会议着实让我兴奋。相关专家们朝着巨大的目标前进，拼命地工作、讨论，感觉自己如同被卷入一个超能量的漩涡中。通过与一起共事的总监们交流，我意识到了总监承担的重要作用。首先是构建景观设计理念，之后是向其他领域的人们说明并让他们理解这个理念。接着需要为具体的空间和形态设计大体框架，推进计划。其二是总监如同掌舵人，需要为手下众多的设计师和技术人员们拟定一个总的工作方向。如果所有的工作都由总监们决定，之后再以此为依据展开工作，就不能形成一种无形的气势。博览会其实就是一种庆典，我意识到，应当让人们愉快地去做他们自己想做的事情。另外，构建并维持人与人之间的关系也是总监的工作。

我在参与这个项目的时候，建筑家菊竹清训团队已制定完会场的总体规划概念。在会场上空25m处建造一个环形木栈道，是在不对地形造成损伤的前提下，确保符合国际规范动线的规划。这与我们这些景观设计师的想法如出一辙。双方拥有共同的理念，共同推进工作的情绪十分高昂。景观在建筑制定场地规划（Site Plan）时介入是项目成功的根源所在。将各区域的建筑群分段，在布局上呈现起伏，并通过地势的高低和斜坡来调整周围的斜坡绿地和池塘等水面之间的等高关系。规划用地位于在日本随处可见、感觉亲和的里山（注：住居附近的群山），因此人们自然会担心这样一个问题：将博览会这样拥有巨大能量的建筑群（象征着城市）嵌入到自然之中是否会对环境产生毁灭性的破坏？我们本着此次世博会的景观设计是解决保存与破坏——"都市和自然之间永恒的主题"这样的信念，推进了整个计划。

世博会场的中心广场正对着日本馆和名古屋市馆，是众多游客聚集之地。在这片场地里，游客们是主角，是"图"；而空间则是支撑这张"图"的"地"。设计中，彻底地执行了这一方针。在单色调的地面铺装中加入埋有瓦片的深灰色条纹，铺装的色调内敛。栽植方面则通过使用大量淡色竹林体现日式风格。用集装箱做的可移动树池，使空间可根据举行活动的要求来变化。早晚不同的阳光照射在突出东西轴线而平铺的瓦片上时，铺装面会呈现不同的表情，

to really study, it is a shame they are letting it pass with time. Opportunities are earned by making effort.

The most largest project since the year 2000, was the task of landscape director for the "Nature's Wisdom" Expo 2005. From starting the project in late 2001 to the last day of exposition on September 30, 2005, I was involved for four years. Not exactly knowing what is the role of a "director" or what was to be done, I literally had to grope my way to begin. The directors meetings were quite an exciting experience for me. There was a gigantic whirl of powerful energy induced by the determined professionals' heated arguments and decisions for the big goal. By discussing with other directors that came into the scene at same time, I became aware of the significant roles as a director. First of all is structuring concept for the landscape design, deliver explanation and seek understanding from the directors of other domains. And then, proceed developing the plan pursued to outlines of specific spaces and forms. Secondly, it is steering the supporting designers and engineers toward the objected direction. If everything was decided at the directors' level and handed down as jobs, the space would end up lacking the vigor it should posses. Exposition is a festival. I realized everybody should pitch in with what they would like and work it out together. And it is the director's responsibility to organize and keep the party in order.

By the time I joined the project, already a master plan concept had been worked out by architect Kiyonori Kikutake's team. It was a plan with a 25 m. width aerial deck surrounding the entire site, without obstructing the geographical features, obtaining universal design accessibilities, perfectly in line with landscape architects' ideologies. Being able to attain mutual respect for each other's concepts, volition to collaborate in achieving the project heightened. Another factor that lead to success was the landscape design participation at the phase of architectural site plan. The architecture groups of each zone were subdivided and arranged in uneven layout, devising ups and downs of ground level with grades, adjustment with the neighboring slopes and water element surfaces were devised. As the planned site situates in a gentle rural landscapc commonly sccn throughout Japan, installing an urban complex like exposition with huge energy involvement, the concern was terminal destruction of the environment. In conviction that the preservation and solution to the "eternal theme of urbanity and nature" is the issue of the landscape design of this exposition, the planning was developed on.

The most central theme zone with Japan Pavilion and Nagoya City Pavilion was conceived to be the most visited area. The design philosophy of this area was the visitors will be the "figures" and the space will be the supporting "ground." In the monotone pavement, dark grey roof tiles were laid in stripes down playing the colors. To feature Japan, plantings were limited to volume of bamboos. The plaza was left open to allow functions with removable containers. The tile stripes emphasizing the east-west direction changing its impression with the sunlight in different time of day was successful in incorporating natural phenomena in the plan （Fig.28）（Fig.29）（Fig.30）（Fig.31）. In the

27 维也纳森柏龙宫殿内的日式庭园（Japanese Garden in the Schonbrunn Palace grounds in Vienna）
28 2005年爱知世博会（Aichi Expo 2005）
29 2005年爱知世博会（Aichi Expo 2005）
30 2005年爱知世博会（Aichi Expo 2005）
31 2005年爱知世博会（Aichi Expo 2005）

成功地将自然的变化引入到规划之中（图28、图29、图30、图31）。在六个月的世博会期间，没有发生大的事故，客流量也大大超过了预期，成功地落下了帷幕。虽然十分劳累，但是通过参与爱·地球博的设计，令我感到自己和人类都拥有无限的可能性，让我对未来充满了希望、生活得非常充实。

在2005年爱·地球博结束之后，我的兴趣开始转向了中国内地。最初在大连和沈阳参与设计了一些工程项目。首先是大连医科大学邀请我去设计景观。日本三井住友建筑公司和建筑家新井清一氏的联合体已在竞标中夺魁。这是个需要考虑如何有机地将景观设计覆盖在原有建筑规划上的项目。规模达110公顷的用地，是一个坐南面海的缓坡，占据绝佳的地理优势。建筑物配置在东西两侧，通过轴线相连，其中间部分为一个大型空间，可以在最大程度上眺望大海。为规划用地中的五个小山丘赋予不同寓意，展开景观设计，对建筑物之间的空间采用柔和的人性化设计，为学生们创造一个恬适的场所。最初还担心整个规划中景观的尺度会过大（over scale），但当看到很多学生都走出校园在这里开展各种活动时，景观的尺度显得适中。在感叹人类的力量的同时，也对这个设计成果放了心。不过有一点可惜的是，由于施工日程较短，影响施工质量，使得设计师的一些意图和对细节的处理没有得到体现；绿化方面也只是栽种了一些瘦弱的树木，要形成一个令人感到自豪的景观还需要等待数年时间（图32、图33、图34）。

沈阳的长白万科城是我在中国第一个独立设计的项目，所以我非常谨慎地推进设计。在中国的住宅区，临街的一侧多被设置成商业街，繁华的商业景观和宁静的住宅景观在这个项目中同时展开。为了让商业街能给寒冷的沈阳带来一丝暖意，对景观构筑物放手地使用了红色和粉色这样的暖色调。住宅区则是一个拥有润泽绿色的空间，儿童游乐场设置其间。居民对绿化的需求大大超乎预计，看来无论哪个国家对亲近自然的渴望都一样。

现在，北京、无锡、苏州、重庆、合肥等地都有项目在运行。在不断遭遇和解决各式各样新课题的过程中，虽然对中国的国情还不是太了解，但是我会与中国的合作者们齐心协力，无论何时，都要努力地创造出美丽的空间（图35、图36）。

six months period, without any drastic accidents, drawing number of visitors higher than had anticipated, the exposition ended with a success. Having participated in "Nature's Wisdom" Expo, although exhausted, I have spent fulfilling and gratifying days having renewed believing in myself, trust in humankind, and that there is still hope for us in the future.

After the "Nature's Wisdom" Expo 2005 was over, my interest have shifted over to continental China. My first step was involving with projects in Dalian and Shenyang. I received an offer in landscape designing for the Dalian Medical University. It was a competition project that Sumitomo Mitui Construction had won with architect Seiichi Arai. It was a project addressing how organically the landscape design could overlay the architecture plan. The site consisting of huge 110 ha was in a splendid location on a gentle southward sloping land. The buildings were laid split into the east and to the west connected by an axis allowing a large open space in between to maximize the view of the sea. The landscape of five slopes within the site were developed with meanings given to each, and between the buildings, a softer design in human scale was applied as relaxing space for the students. There was a concern that the landscape design being over scaled; nevertheless, once the student body was on campus resuming about their activities, it all appeared to be in right scale. I was impressed by the power that radiates off people and at the same time relieved the application went well. Unfortunately, however, due to not having had enough time, construction level is poor not reflecting enough of the designer's intentions and details as well as the trees brought in were much smaller than what had been proposed. It would take some years for the landscape to become one to take pride in （Fig.32）（Fig.33）（Fig.34）.

As the Changbai Vanke project in Shenyang was my very first project in China, I resumed planning with absolute attentiveness. As it is common in China to build shops along the street side of collective housings, a bright and gay shopping landscape and a quieter residential landscape were simultaneously designed. In the shopping area, warm colors of red and pink sculptures were installed to bring some warm feeling to the cold Shenyang country. The residential area was adorned with peaceful lush greenery with children's active play lot. The residents had requested for more plants than I had assumed which gave me an understanding that to wish to be close to nature is universal.

Currently, the projects in Beijing, Wuxi and Amoy （Xiamen） are in progress. New issues arise with each project, and solving it one by one takes a long period of time that at this moment the goals are still in the obscure horizon. Nevertheless, working close together with the collaborators in China, I intend to continue to create beautiful long lasting landscapes （Fig.35）（Fig.36）.

32 大连医科大学（Dalian Medical University）
33 大连医科大学（Dalian Medical University）
34 大连医科大学（Dalian Medical University）
35 沈阳长白万科城（Shenyang Changbai Wanke City）
36 沈阳长白万科城（Shenyang Changbai Wanke City）

"Symbiosis of nature and city" was the theme of this project plan, but it may be easier to grasp should the word "city" be replaced with "people". Even without visiting any of the attractions inside the pavilions, by just walking around the 2.6km encircling pedestrian deck, people may have felt sense of overwhelm by the subtle beauty of Japan Plaza or soothed by the natural landscape of Satoyama, It is wished that the ideology of Expo which brought man and nature closer will be passed on to the many generations to come.

2005 年 爱 · 地球博的景观设计

"Nature's Wisdom" EXPO 2005

2005 年 爱 · 地球博的景观设计
Nagakute, Aichi, 2005

　　历经数次园艺博览会，日本的园林设计和园艺技术都已达到引领世界潮流的水准。日本人对自然细致入微的关爱和接触方式，在园艺世界如同盛开的鲜花绽放。但是，这次爱·地球博的规划用地有别于围合式庭园化的园艺博览会，是在开放的自然之中展现城市生活和文化的一块试验田。作为景观设计的负责人，如何将人工建造的城市融入自然，如何布置设施才能不给人们造成压迫感，这些都让我和事务所的同仁绞尽脑汁。

　　会场的规划理念——环球圈（Global Rope）和地球村的思想和设计，顺利地反映在景观设计之中，并使之提升到另一个高度。位于丘陵低洼深处的展示区域，向内侧地势呈上扬趋势，调整了人们的视觉。为了减缓建筑体量带来的压迫感，利用高低变换对建筑物进行了布置。背景林显现在建筑物的间隔之中，相对于池水水面将周边的地形设置得稍低，以此让地形和树林形成一体。这些都让我对景观设计之中布置地形规划的重要性有了一个全新的认识。

　　2005 年日本世博广场是以游客的活动为主体的"图"，景观为"地"展开的设计。在日本广场单色调的地面铺装之中加入石板和瓦片形成深灰色的条纹，植栽方面也减少色彩的使用，通过竹林的绿与量衬托广场。瓦片铺装构成了广场东西轴线，在早晚不同阳光的照射下，向人们展现出不同的表情；它引导人们的视线越过轴线上生物肺（Bio Lunge）的高大乔木，指向"海上森林"。

　　空间和形态作为设计行为的主流思想已众所周知。如今，我们已经认识到，人类到了去关注、接受身边仅存的自然，并长久与其共存下去的最后关头。相信被喻为环境博览会，并冠以"自然的睿智"主题的爱·地球博，作为人类和自然共存的试验田，一定能向世人传递这个信息。

Japanese landscape design and gardening technologies have rose to a world leading level through several gardening Expos. It seems Japanese sensibilities towards nature and wild life came to bloom in the horticultural society. However, unlike the previous horticultural gardening expositions, the Aichi Expo was an experiment to express contemporary urban life and culture within unfolded nature. As the landscape design director, the effort was made in how to incorporate urbanity into nature and layout the facilities without coercive impression.

The concept and design ideologies, "Global Loop" and "Global Common" were easily adapted and emphasized in the landscape design. For the Commons in the basins, the angle of the slope was increased gradually towards the depths for visual effect. To avoid exposing volumes of architectures, the buildings were positioned inconsistently, making the trees in the rear visible in between, and by lowering the ground level against the water surface, integration of the surrounding trees and topographical features were devised. These efforts renewed our perception of its significance in landscape designs.

The open spaces were designed as the "ground" for the activities of the visitors as the "figure." Japan Plaza was composed of monotone paving with dark gray stripes of stones and tiles, limiting colors of plants, and massive volume of bamboos. The tile paving in east-west axis reflecting sunlight showing different expressions in mornings and evenings, and guiding the eyes along the axis beyond the tall trees of the Bio-Lung Tower to the Kaisho no Mori（forest above the sea）.

There is no doubt that space and forms are the main streams of our landscape design process. Nevertheless, it is our mutual understanding that we are today at a crucial stage to take account of what is left of our natural environment and must aspire to its sustaining. Referred as an environmental exposition, with theme of "Nature's Wisdom", the Expo was an experiment of symbiosis of man and nature. We trust we were able to deliver a message for the future generations.

对面页：会场中心的日本广场

日本馆、名古屋市馆、日本广场

人们大都喜欢面向池塘的开阔空间。因此，在池塘背后的连续悬挑的平台之下设置了观众席以便观看在下方池塘中举办的活动。在作为南北轴线的地面铺装中，使用白色系的鲜明线条；而东西轴线的地面铺装中则埋入瓦片，使用略暗的低色调作为线条。早晚各异的阳光照射在东西轴线上时，瓦片也会反射出不同的光线，形成了一种能够表现其存在感的独特氛围。

People tend to prefer openness of the space facing the pond. In beyond is the aerial deck with spectator seats built below for watching the events at the pond. The north-south axis is emphasized by bright white line in the pavement while the east-west axis line in tiles of low-toned colors. The reflection of sunlight against the tiles appearing in the east-west axis in the mornings and the evenings was effective in achieving an accentuated ambience.

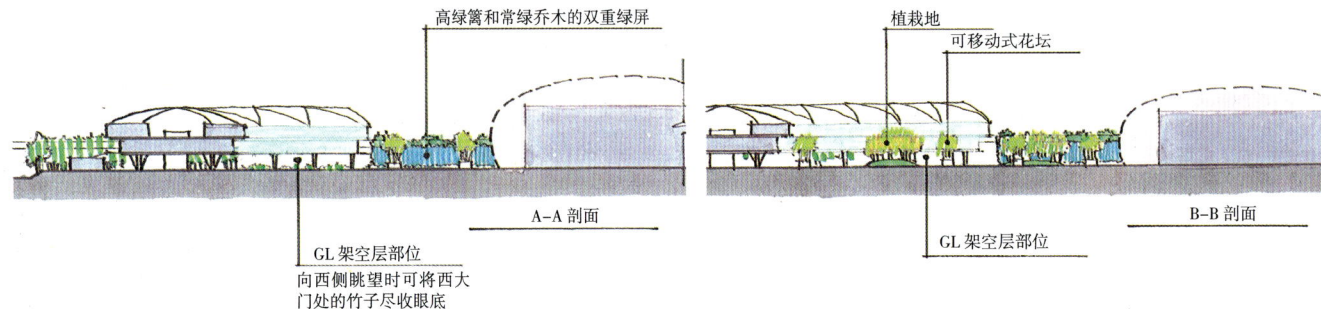

高绿篱和常绿乔木的双重绿屏

A-A 剖面

GL 架空层部位
向西侧眺望时可将西大门处的竹子尽收眼底

植栽地
可移动式花坛

B-B 剖面

GL 架空层部位

用于日本广场中的再生瓦片的平板铺装

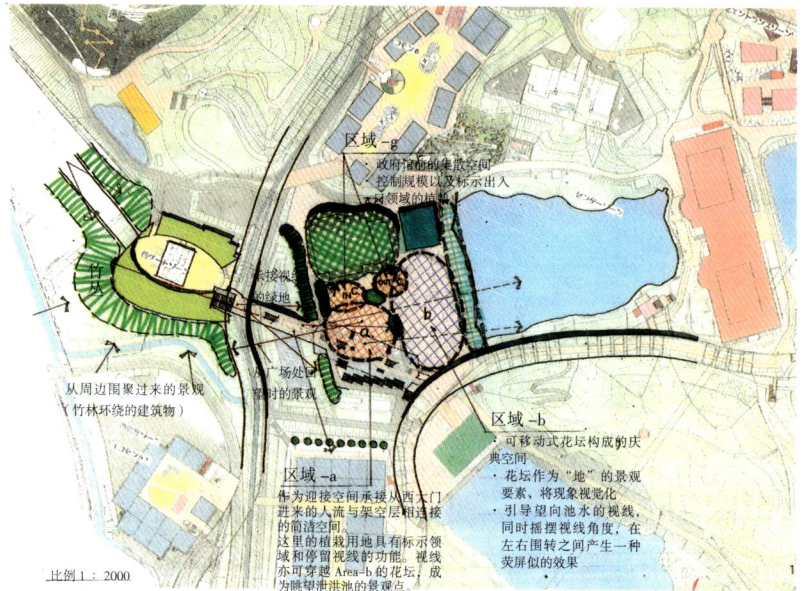

区域-g
· 政府窗前的集散空间
· 控制规模以及标示出入
· 同领域的植栽

从周边围聚过来的景观
（竹林环绕的建筑物）

广场处
窗时的蒙茸

区域-a
作为迎接空间承接从西大门
进来的人流与架空层相连接
的简洁空间。
这里的植栽用地具有标示领
域和停留视线的功能。视线
亦可穿越 Area-b 的花坛，成
为眺望泄洪池的景观点。

区域-b
· 可移动式花坛构成的庆
典空间
· 花坛作为"地"的景观
要素，将现象视觉化
· 引导望向池水的视线，
同时摇摆视线角度，在
左右围转之间产生一种
荧屏似的效果

比例 1：2000

西大门至入口区域·空间构成图

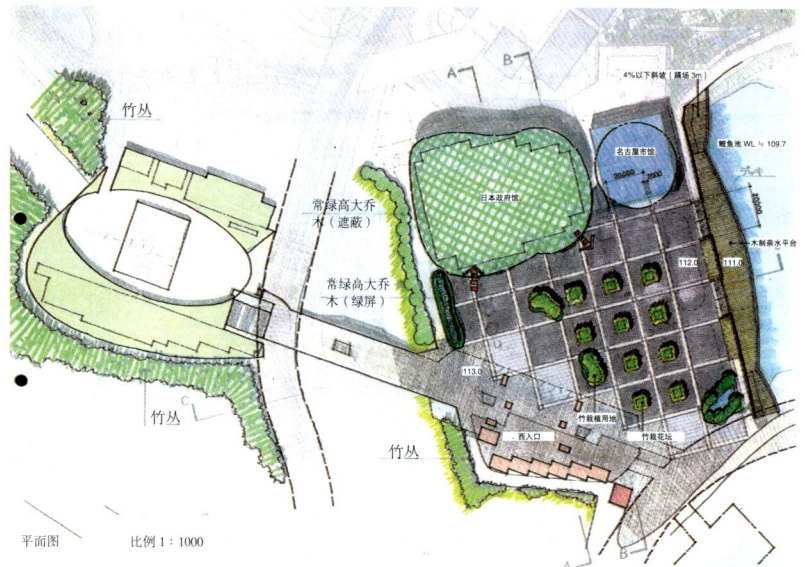

竹丛

常绿高大乔
木（遮蔽）

常绿高大乔
木（绿屏）

竹丛

竹丛

平面图   比例 1：1000

西大门至入口·日本区平面图

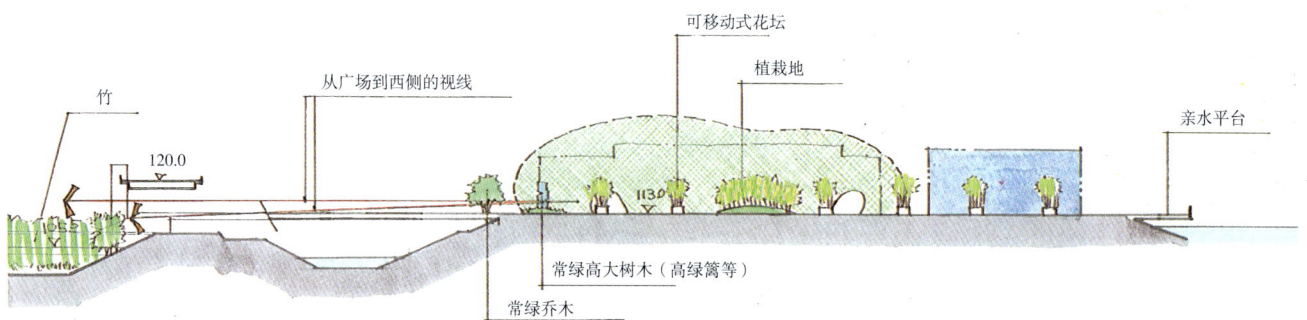

可移动式花坛

植栽地

竹

从广场到西侧的视线

亲水平台

120.0

常绿高大树木（高绿篱等）

常绿乔木

剖面图

广场椅凳空间以能联想到日本风格的竹为素材，简洁的框架可作为多功能的景观小品。一部分树坛拆分为4块，用铲车把它们运至四周，腾让出宽广的活动空间。会议期间，花钵在园艺师们举办的反映季节变化的花卉种植（Installation）活动中大显身手。

Bamboos, symbolizing Japan, with various simple structure frames were installed as diverse stage sets in the sitting area of the wide plaza. Some of the planters were disassembled into four parts and removed out by forklifts to make space for larger functions. Flower artists applied seasonal installation to the planter.

■ 重量计算
竹: 60kg/m×5m=300kg
土: 2.4×0.7×1.8t/m³=3.0t   合计 3.5 t
树池: 200kg
坐凳: 200kg

■坐凳·花坛分离

铲斗
重心
铲斗开幅
铲车载重 4t

铲平 4 吨级

合计重量 3.5 t

■平面图   Plan 1:50

■草图

■立面图   Elevation 1:50

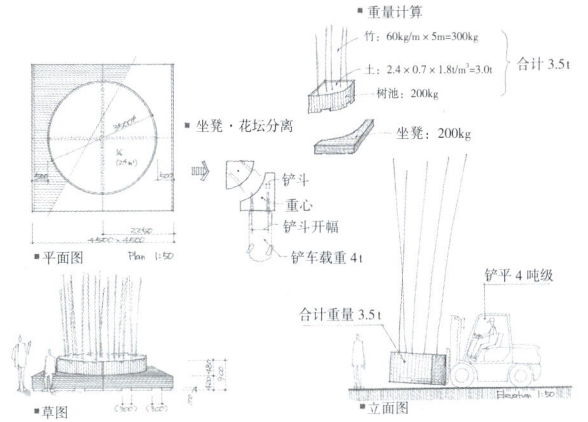

日本广场   可动式树坛方案

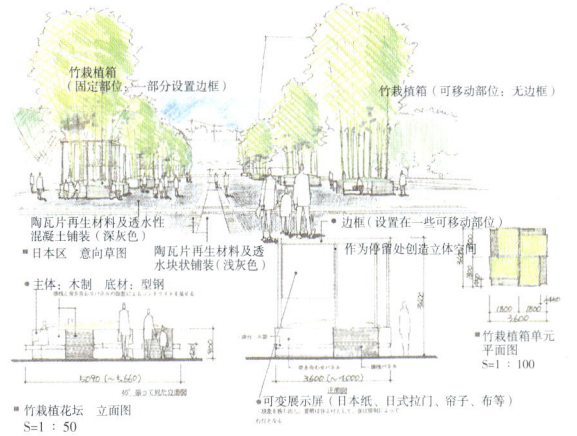

竹栽植箱
(固定部位:一部分设置边框)

竹栽植箱
(可移动部位:无边框)

陶瓦片再生材料及透水性
混凝土铺装(深灰色)

■ 日本区   意向草图

■ 主体:木制   底材:型钢

■竹栽植花坛   立面图
S=1:50

陶瓦片再生材料及透
水块状铺装(浅灰色)

边框(设置在一些可移动部位)
作为停留处创造立体空间

■可变展示屏(日本纸、日式拉门、帘子、布等)

竹栽植箱单元
平面图
S=1:100

日本区广场规划方案

连接空中木栈道的斜坡

空中木栈道风景

亚洲区入口

从西口的空中木栈道处观望草坪广场

西口的餐厅区

空中木栈道行驶的自行车 Taxi

LOOP 规划方案

周长 2.6 公里的悬挑平台上规划建造高低差在 40 米、5% 以下的无障碍坡道。通过这个平台可以快速到达会场内任何一个展馆，是会场内最重要的设施。并且，从这个平台上所看到的连续景观的变化被绘制成草图，最终成为研讨景观控制的参考图。

The aerial deck circling the length of 2.6km was designed with less than 5% slope for the 40m level variations creating a smooth accessing system. This deck allowed people to easily access all pavilions and is the most important facility of the EXPO. The sketches below are the case study of the landscape sequences viewed from the deck.

由于规划用地的地势起伏较大，所以肯定会留下很多人造斜坡（西大门处）。在博览会期间，用大量的花草植被覆盖地面，既美化了景观也给游客一种赏心悦目之感。

The planned site had undulating topographical feature, therefore it was inevitable to incorporate the existing landforms (west gate). In the duration of the EXPO, abundance of attractive flowers and foliage groundcovers were planted to appease the visitors.

将河边的一部分混凝土护岸改造成原生态护岸，从而形成一个符合环境博览会主题的空间，采用石头堆造的两段式结构，可供丰水期时使用。后方遮阳棚的创意来自于枫树的果实。

In creating an amicable space to the Expo theme, the concrete embankment was modified to natural style embankment with two- story stone structure in prediction of high water level. The shelter in the background is designed in a "maple key" motif.

与日本广场相邻的大花坛设想成是世博会的吉祥物居住的森林和开花的田野。同时，通过在关键场所布置的人工造型的树木和竹笼这种日本传统工艺品，给人们一种置身里山的感觉。

The large flowerbed next to the Japan Plaza was designed in an image of flower garden and forest where mascot character of Expo lives. With topiaries and traditional bamboo craft basket, a rural village landscape of Japan is expressed.

各个展馆建筑本身都能够将各国的特点鲜明地表现出来，即便只是在区域内行走，也可以乐在其中。大陆被分为6大板块，在各个板块的中心都设置了可以进行多种活动的空间，并尽量减少景观小品的设置。

It was enjoyable just to walk around the pavilions with attractive architectures displaying cultural characteristics of each country. The area having divided into 6 continental zones, landscape design elements were kept minimal to make ample space available for variety of events.

印度、希腊、乌克兰等国的展馆

日本庭园的设计立足于传统，大胆地使用了当地的石料作为竖立的石块，并提出了一种新的庭园设计思路。通过竖立的石块、雾与河流，创造出幻想般的空间。旋转涌动的水流之中蕴含着一种时尚感。

While the Zen garden was designed in traditional method, with dynamic use of local stones, it is proposing a new direction of Zen gardens. The effect of standing stones, the stream and the drifting mist is of a remote ambience. Swirling water stream within its modern image bear obscurity.

漩涡状流水

最深处的瀑布和雾

瀑布和流水

林中茶室

下图是观赏池塘景观的观众席。楼梯上方的座位在展会结束之后会栽种树木，预计 5 年后可以高过人头。通过这种设计，可以让观众席重新回归到自然森林之中。

The renderings below show spectator seats by the pond. The plan was to bed plantings on the upper level of the stairs after the festival closed. In 5 years time, the trees will grow over human height and return to natural forest.

世博会期间的阶梯，25 年后将成为森林。

北美洲展区

基 · 地 · 图

其实这个聚集众多游客的节日会场，在半年里都是一个临时的、幻想之中的空间。一般来说，日常的景观设计通常以丰富的自然背景作为"地"，人工设计的景观作为"图"，两者组合，形成风景。但是这次，当接触了许多随心所欲的游乐于会场之中的游客之后，我的想法改变了。真正的"图"应该是人类的行为，而支撑这一行为的各种设计才应该是"地"。而让这一切都能够得到实现的水流、森林和山丘等则可以被称为"基"。因为有了自然恩惠的"基"，人类才能发挥自己的睿智，设计了"地"这样的空间，然后充分享受并使用这些空间的人们又形成了"图"，这样一想，就应该可以更加深刻地理解人类和自然之间的关系了。

"Base", "Ground" and "Figure"

The venue of this monumental festival was a half-year provisional and fictional space. It is an understanding in landscape design, the lush background nature is assumed as the "Ground" and the designed elements as the "Figure," and scenery is made from the combinations. However, in observing the visitors moving around enjoying in their own ways, it became aware that the true "Figure" was the human activities, and the various design elements are the supporting "Ground." And the basic elements as the water, the woods and the slopes should be called the "Base." In defining the natural blessings as the "Base," and establishing human creations as the "Ground," where people as the "Figure" enjoy upon, the relationship of human and nature may be come clearer.

不同的新兴风景，从而使度假空间的价值得以凸显。下面列举五个富有特色的设施群实例。由于参观者会在那里度过特定的时间，给人留下强烈印象的设计也是一种有效的方法。 这里介绍的空间是由花、昆虫、农业、温室、日本庭园等易于理解的常见设施构成，满足了参观者的不同需求。

The prerequisite for a successful resort space is the location. If the landscape design could be developed incorporating the landscape of the location as borrowed or even contained scenery, a new out-of-everyday landscape will be born and will enhance the value of the resort.

Introduced here are five projects with characteristic facilities. As the users will be spending some time at the location, applying impressive plans is an effective method. Here, the landscape is composed around graspable elements as flowers, insects, farming, greenhouse, and Japanese gardens, and responding to the users' various needs.

群马昆虫之林

羽生农林公园

向岛洋兰中心

谷川仙寿庵

梦之岛热带植物馆

Gunma Insects World

群马昆虫之林

Kiryu, Gunma, 2006

　　"群马昆虫之林"是日本第一个以野地（Field）为主体的昆虫观察设施。规划用地面积约为48公顷，由四个区域构成。对既存里山环境进行保护和再生而形成的杂树林、桑田、里山水田这三个区域之外，还有对垃圾填埋工程等形成的荒地进行复原和新建的园地——富士山湿地区域。群马昆虫之林为人们提供一个亲近里山多彩的自然、与那里的生物共处的场所。

　　在生态学家所给出的环境调查和环境论证的基础之上，将生态和利用生态的内容与环境的再生修复规划的内容整合在一起，并且和硬件设施设计一起实施，从而对后山环境进行保护和再生。在杂树林区域，通过更新和改良树林地面来提高生态环境的质量，并建立观察点或是开辟林间小道，让人们可以接触到各种生物。在桑田区域，通过对移筑的赤城型民宅的庭院前空间、果树园和桑田等进行的二次修整，创造出一个既可以体验传统农业又可以接触各种生物的场所。

　　富士山湿地区域设置了昆虫观察馆，整个项目的核心设施的展示内容围绕着放蝶温室和昆虫世界两个主题构成。在设计上，通过与建筑设计师的反复协商，成功地将建筑物与其周边园地紧密地联系在一起。例如，由入口一直到观察馆，所有的建筑都被里山所环绕，形成了一种若隐若现的连续景观；有意识地将地形与建筑联系在一起；将建筑引入其中的水景或是将里山风景等如同宽银幕一般进行展现。野地里努力营造出这样一种环境——通过生态复原技术对里山中具有代表性的环境进行布景，使那些原本对生物和自然不感兴趣的游客，也能在里山中轻易地接触到大自然，并将这种感触与自己在观察馆中所获取的信息和体验结合起来。此外，导入了纵断各个区域的多姿多彩的水系，让其作为主导环境要素。除了地表水，还将规划用地的潜流也引入总体系之中，形成了一种十分接近自然的水流体系，再将它与周边的农业水系联系起来，成功地实现了徜徉在地域生态之中的里山水系。

Gunma Insect World is Japan's very first field facility establishment for the study of insects. The 48ha park site is composed of four distinctive zones; revived rural village landscape of coppice, mulberry farm, rice field, and Mt. Fuji marsh zone restored from reclaimed wasteland, providing a wild life experience in a vast natural environment.

For preservation of rural environment, founding on surveys and assessments by ecology specialists, ecology and activities program, and planning of preservation and restoration conformed to the program, and designing of the hardware were done. In the forest zone, renewal and maintenance of the forest bed for ecological quality improvement, and observation points and trail plans were executed. For the mulberry farm, a garden space around the relocated old silk-raising farmhouse, the farm, and orchard were fixed for a field experience of traditional farming and natural life.

The Fuji mountain marsh zone locates the core facility of the park, insect observation pavilion with exhibitions the thematic world of insects, and greenhouse where butterflies are freed. In the process of site planning, numerous discussions with the architects took place as to the sequence of view through rural landscape from the entrance to the main pavilion, the layout of architectures in relation to the geographical features, and the panorama view of the architecture against the water and rural landscape in order to create intimate relation of the architecture and the park site. By introduction of ecology preservation technologies, typical rural environment was recreated in effort to readily connect knowledge acquired at the pavilion and the actual experience of nature in the field even for the visitors with less interest in wildlife. Additionally, as a structural environmental element, diverse water channels were devised to run through the zones. Incorporating rainwater to the water supply, a system close to a river was realized, and by joining the system with the neighboring farmland, the coming and goings of the wildlife of the region was made possible.

对面页：昆虫森林的前奏空间，等待迎接人们的森林。

连成年人进入森林时都兴奋不已，就更不用说孩子们了，他们肯定希望能在这里奔跑。为了承载人们的兴奋之情，在大门口安置了十分有力度的堆石，围合成大弧度的园路。让人们在出发地点也能够看见前行者的身影，这一点十分重要。

It is always exciting to enter into a forest. For children it may be more so urging them to dash in. As to respond to the heightened mood, a dynamic stonewall and a wide curving trail entrance were staged. It is also effective to be able to see the people walking ahead.

入口通道

从入口处眺望停车场

温室由安藤忠雄设计。建筑整体由一种令人联想到梯田的两段水面构成，与山脊共同形成了一幅天际美景。建筑物大型屋顶下方的外部阶梯还是可以举办各种活动的空间。

The atrium is of Tadao Ando's design. The architecture has a sloping skyline representing mountain ridge, and composed with a double layer of water surface in the image of rice paddies. The external stairs under a large roof is a space made available for various functions.

"群马昆虫之林"总平面图

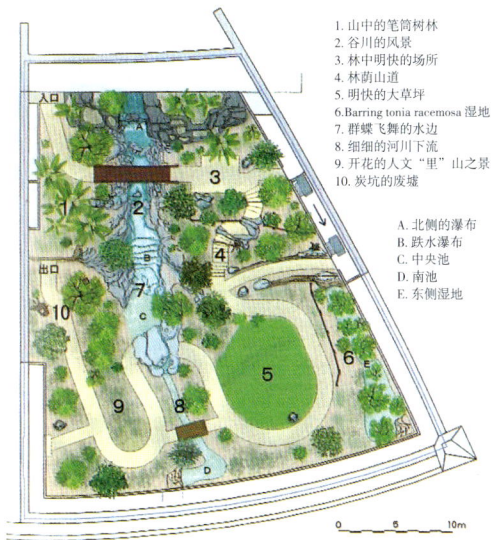

1. 山中的笔筒树林
2. 谷川的风景
3. 林中明快的场所
4. 林荫山道
5. 明快的大草坪
6. Barring tonia racemosa 湿地
7. 群蝶飞舞的水边
8. 细细的河川下流
9. 开花的人文"里"山之景
10. 炭坑的废墟

A. 北侧的瀑布
B. 跌水瀑布
C. 中央池
D. 南池
E. 东侧湿地

森林生态温室以再现冲绳地区的生态和风景为目的而建造。那里栽种了冲绳地区的植物，设有瀑布、河流与池塘，是一个昆虫生态的展示空间。在温室内飞舞的蝴蝶经常使游客们为之欢呼雀跃，让人们感受到一种不同寻常的乐趣。

The forest ecology greenhouse objected to reproduce ecology and landscape of Okinawa. Using plants of Okinawa and water to create waterfall, cascade and pond as a space for insect's ecological exhibition. The visitors shout in joy to the flock of butterflies and seem to enjoy out-of-ordinary experiences in the greenhouse.

对富士山湿地区域的填埋垃圾荒地进行了复原和新建工作。在该区域设置水流与池塘、建造绿地广场，使其成为一个可以让孩子们进行观察生态以及自由活动的场所。通过在岸边建造木制平台来设置散步道及小空间，形成一个亲水景观。

The barren land resulting from reclamation was restored as Mt. Fuji Marsh zone with stream, pond, and grassland for the children's ecology observation and activities. For easy access to the water, wooden decks, pedestrian paths, and small open areas are laid close to water.

采集昆虫的孩子们

各区域主要断面图

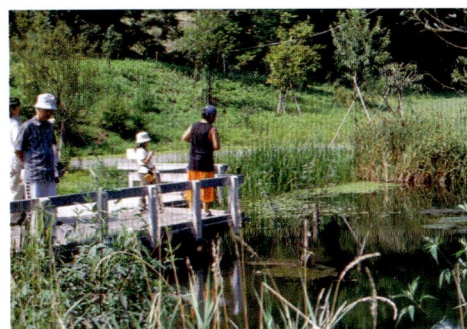

虽然是一个新建的空间，但是只要考虑生态，用自
然的园路处理好和周边的关系，可以给人一种由来
已久的感觉。

Although it is a newly constructed space, by taking
ecological measures to fuse the trail with the
surrounding environment, it is possible to create an
atmosphere that the landscape had existed from long
before.

在杂树林和里山水田区域之中，只设置了最小限度的园路，仅供观察所用，从而达到保护自然的目的。不过也会在那些很有特色的风景或是昆虫观察点附近刻意设置凳椅，通过柔和弯曲的园路让人们享受到连续性景观的乐趣。

To protect natural environment, the trail for observation were kept to minimum in the village zone and through the thickets. However, in scenic points bench seats were installed to manipulate awareness, and gentle curving trail lead through the sequences of sceneries.

自古以来，人类的生活就与昆虫密不可分。尤其是能吐生丝的蚕所形成的产业，更是农家的收入之源。所以，对古民宅移筑区域的桑田和果树园进行了整治，创造出一个可以让游客体验古代农业的空间。

There is a long history of insects tied to our lives. For instance, silkworm, which produces raw silk, was an industry and farmers' income source. In the zone where the old dismantled home is rebuilt, mulberry farm and orchard were restored to allow the visitors experience agricultural life of the old days.

生态

距今30年前的那段时期，人们的住所附近有许多昆虫，收集和观察它们都只是一些日常的活动。但是现在，人们却只能在远离都市的森林中进行这种活动。想在杉树林那样的人造森林中发现各种生物或是昆虫根本就不可能。"群马昆虫之林"就是在这样的情况下落成了。愿人们能更接近、感受生物的多样性，并把人类生活与昆虫之间的密切关系一直延续到下一代。

Ecology

About thirty years ago, there were a lot of insects found in the neighborhood of our lives, and collecting and studying them were part of our daily life. However, today, it is necessary to travel away from urban environment to the forests. Even so, it is impossible to find various wild life and insects in secondary forests. That is why, "Gunma Insects World" came to being, but hopefully, biodiversity could be experienced in and around our lives again, and relation of human race and insects sustain on to the next generation.

Kiyasse-Hanyu

羽生农林公园
Hanyu, Saitama, 2001

"合作"（Cooperation）这个词已耳熟能详。推进一项事业，毋庸置疑需要各种各样的人和组织间的配合，强调合作重要性的呼声也非常强烈。一项事业需要通过横向讨论——各领域的设计师和技术人员跨越自己本职进行交流，与垂直行为——各领域的设计师和技术人员完成自己的实际工作，才能得以完成。

羽生农林公园规划就是以总指挥北山孝雄为中心，通过建筑家北山孝二郎和我们景观设计小组之间的通力合作，共同完成的项目。这里，首要考虑的是：如何实现建筑与景观设计的一体化。

作为用地规划，将建筑敞向四周的风景，在中庭设置热闹的广场和草坪，并通过内侧那座具有象征意义的山丘来引导人们的视线。建筑物的大型屋顶向外下斜延伸至广场，环抱着风景，尽显力度，与周围的环境相互协调的同时显示着自身的存在性。通过山丘和河流，将这块土地所蕴含的历史和文化悄无声息地表现出来。在充实设施利用内容之后，上述空间才得以真正地展现。

在深化研讨软件与硬件的过程中，适合各个不同专业技术的空间得以完成。这个成果更加坚定了相互间今后继续合作的意志。

The word "collaboration" has been generally used for quite sometime. Needless to say, in order to proceed on an enterprise, supports from many individuals and/or organizations are inevitable, and in recent years, essentiality of collaboration is being more called for. An enterprise is materialized by task assigned designers and engineers discussing, in various stages of the project, on equal horizontal terms in achieving vertical objective.

This project was realized with Takao Kitayama as the producer, and in collaborating effort between architect Kojiro Kitayama and our landscape architect team. The most deliberation was given on expressing a sense of unity of architecture and landscape.

As for the site plan, architectures were arranged to spread out in the open landscape with an activity space and grass lawn in the courtyard, and a symbolical hill was created in the far end of the site for visionary effect. The massive roof of the architecture extends out over the plaza incorporating the landscape dynamically, asserting its existence in harmonious manner to the surrounding. The historical and cultural contexts of the region are represented in the hill and the canals. Spatial expressions become only effective with enrichment of activity programs.

The accomplished space, responding to the high professional qualities in line to the comprehensive discussions over the software and hardware, owes solely to the unyielding efforts of the collaborating team.

对面页：位于公园中心处小丘的顶部，用日本辛夷树修饰休憩空间。

从入口正面向内观望的风景是规划中最为重要的一部分。由大型屋顶所构成的朝向建筑群的轴线，遮掩着背后的开放性空间，若隐若现，具有激发游客热情的效果。

One of the most significant features of the project is the scenery from the entrance gate. On the axis line leading towards the architectures with massive roofs, glimpses of the backdrop landscape can be observed for the effect of raising visitors' anticipations.

水与大体量的建筑物尤为般配。建筑物的倒影映照在水面，随风而动、泛起的涟漪勾画出动态风景。

Water surface enhance large scaled buildings. The reflections in the water transform itself by the wind caused rippling of waves creating a landscape with movements.

在餐厅前设置一个开放式的平台，乔木的阴影展现出深邃的风景。

Front of the restaurant is made into an open terrace, and the shades created by the trees add depth to the scenery.

放置在户外的商品可以激发出场地的活力，为风景增添乐趣。

Merchandises crowded out of the shops add liveliness and merriment to the landscape.

山丘上设置了一个木制平台，既可观赏风景又可休息。主景树选用了枝叶分布均衡、冠形优美的树木。

A wooden deck was constructed on the hilltop as a resting place to enjoy the view. A tree with ample width and handsome features was selected as a landmark tree.

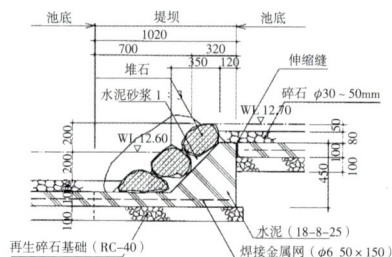

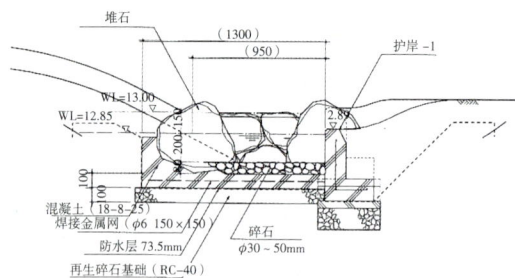

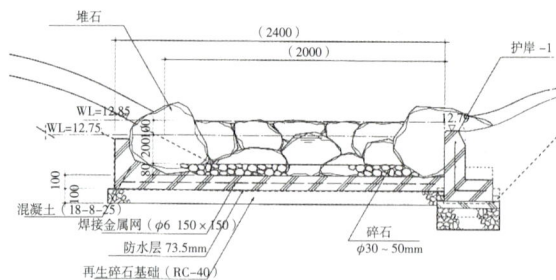

将公园的一角建设为生态空间。这里曾经是湿地，水位至今仍然很高，在此充分利用水，为孩子们创造了一个学习环境知识的场所。木制平台引导游客自然走向水边，深受游客们的喜爱。

Biotope was installed in a corner of the park. The site area had been a marshland still having high water level today. Utilizing the abundant supply of water, a children's ecology education ground was facilitated. Wooden deck ideally serves the purpose of guiding people close to the water and is being popularly used.

针对建筑颇具力度的造型，采用了简洁的景观设计。例如，只在小桥的单侧设置扶手，站在桥上眺望景色显得空旷、深邃。

In contrast to the dynamic appearance of the architectures, the landscape was designed in simple composition. The bridge has handrail only on one side allowing spacious view across the water.

水景

如何运用好"水"这一要素，对于景观设计来说是一个重要的课题。水，不仅能为风景增添变化，而且导入水，可以带来凉意，捎来一缕缕轻风。另外，"水"作为生命之源，还拥有吸引鸟类和昆虫等各种生命体的能力。这些东西的集合体只存在我们所居住的地球，持续不断地创建这些小小的空间是我们景观设计师的职责所在。刚开始它可能只是一个点，但是渐渐地会成为一条线，然后形成一个面，并在真正意义上使我们的生活变得丰富多彩。

Waterscape

Skillful use of "water" is one of the most important themes in landscape architecture. The water not only transforms the scenery, but also draws in fresh air and cause gentle breeze. Moreover, "water" being the source of life attracts birds and insects, the wildlife. Such symbiotic assemblage is no other than the Earth we live on, and it could be said that it is the responsibility of the landscape architects to continue to create these small communities. The beginning may be just a dot, but it will eventually grow into a line and into a plane, and will bring true richness to our lives.

通过对地形、设施和植物的组合，制定一个丰富多彩而又富有深度的规划。水面和小桥的水平线、山丘的柔和曲线与树木的垂直线条共同构建了让人百看不厌的风景。

It is possible to plan depth and diversity in a landscape by overlaying landforms, facilities, and greenery. Enduring landscape was composed with horizontal line of water surface and bridge, gentle curving line of the hill, and the vertical line of the trees.

Mukaishima Orchid Center

向岛洋兰中心
Mukaishima, Hiroshima, 1995

洋兰中心的中央庭园及其周边景观感动着来访的游客。位于建筑南侧的庭园面积宽广（大约4000m²），其中央有一个圆形的绿地广场（直径50m）。这个草坪广场除了可以供人散步和慢跑之外，还可以用来举办室外音乐会等各种各样的活动，被市民们称为新型庭园。

这个庭园的景观采用借景的手法将周边的山景引入其中，形成了简洁、赋有力度感的近代回游庭园。水系和园路为主要构架。从当地挖掘出的巨石上部的凹处，水如同涌泉般流出，落地后形成水流，勾画出一道曲线，流淌到上部水池中。在那里，水流转化成瀑布，流淌过小桥，缓缓地、蜿蜒地穿行过草坪，流入下部主池。自始至终周边的群山环绕着水流，水似山中来的景色展现在人们的眼前。

自建筑处延伸而来的主园路呈半圆形并慢慢抬高，渐渐地融入背后的群山之中。这样可以达到如下效果：背景与园内的风景无限接近，赋予空间深邃感与宽广感，孕育一种非景观设计不达的庭园与地域一体化的美妙空间。

The center garden of Mukaishima Orchid Center, along with its surrounding landscape, strikes the visitors with a sense of awe. The garden located in the south of the architecture has a wide open space (approx. 4000m²) and a circular grass lawn (50m diameter) in its center. This circular plaza is used for strolling, jogging as well as variety of events as music concerts, and is being recognized as a new type of garden by the citizens.

The landscape of this garden incorporates surrounding mountains as "shakkei: borrowed scenery," and designed as a simple and dynamic modern strolling garden. The framework of the design is water canals and paths. The water canal begins springing from a hollow of a large rock dug from the site ground, overflows into a stream, and in winding sweeps, into the upper pond. From there it cascades down under a bridge, and meanders through the lawn and flows into lower main pond. The layers of mountains in the backdrop unfold a landscape as if the water had come from the mountains.

The main path from the side of the building winds in half circle in gradual slope fuses into the mountains. As a result, the background and the garden are integrated, creating depth and width of the space. A landscape design in a true sense of embodiment of garden and the surrounding area was achieved.

对面页：舒缓、流畅的水与线条优美的园路，背景植物群落体量适宜。

将周边的标志性物体融入景观设计之中非常重要。展现与远方电视塔相连的"水流"，设置将人们的视线导向附近的大型乔木，努力使景观与周边一体化。

It is important to incorporate landmarks of the area into the landscape. By expressing "water flow" as if it continues onto a television tower at a far distance, or guiding the eyes in the direction of large trees in the neighboring land, integration of the surrounding landscape is attempted.

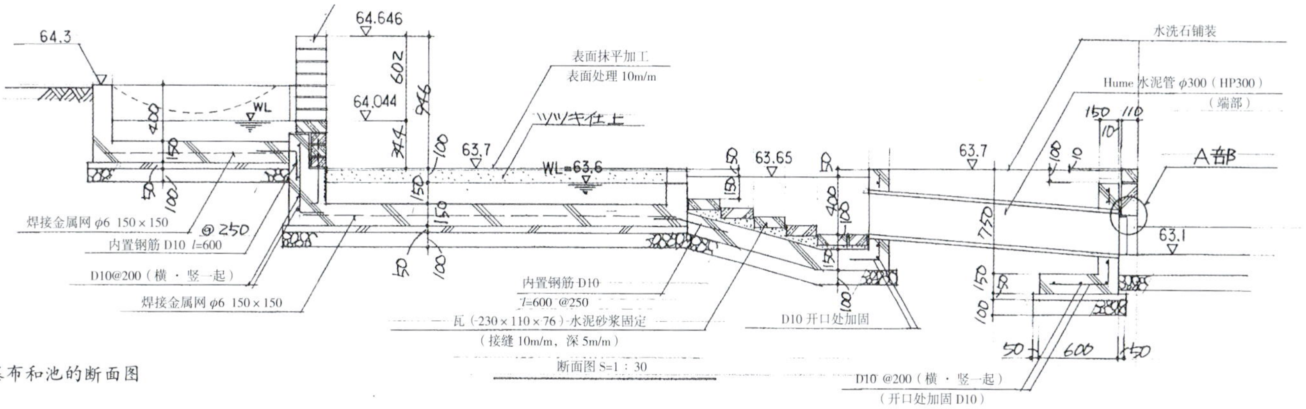

64.3

64.646

64.044

表面抹平加工
表面处理 10m/m

ツツキ仕上

WL=63.6

63.7

63.7

水洗石铺装

Hume 水泥管 φ300（HP300）
（端部）

A部B

63.65

63.1

焊接金属网 φ6 150×150

内置钢筋 D10 l=600

D10@200（横・竖一起）

焊接金属网 φ6 150×150

内置钢筋 D10
l=600 @250

瓦（-230×110×76）水泥砂浆固定
（接缝 10m/m，深 5m/m）

断面图 S=1：30

D10 开口处加固

D10 @200（横・竖一起）
（开口处加固 D10）

63.7

瀑布和池的断面图

桥是衔接空间的有效手段。在连接的同时，桥也是转换人
们意识的一种设施。由此，应作为景观的重要因素加以运用。

宽广的草坪配以简洁、弯曲的水流，尽显力度。

The water canal drawing a dynamic simple curving line in the wide lawn space.

小桥和广场部分是这个庭园设计中唯一使用直线的部分，作为建筑性要素融入周边环境之中。小桥的扶手采用点缀性色彩漆成红色，与周围的绿色形成鲜明对比。

The bridge and its landing is the only element designed in straight lines casting architectural features to the area. The red color of the bridge railing as an accent strikes a contrast to the greenery of the surrounding.

草坪广场砖瓦桥的断面图

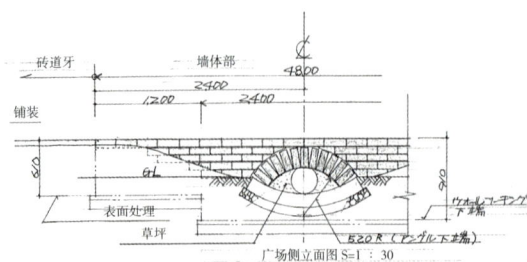

池塘作为建筑和庭园的连接点，不但保证了室内良好的采光，还可将粼粼水光反射到室内的顶棚上。池塘周边种植了大量地被植物，植物和水相结合，细部也尽显温馨。

As the pond was made the element to link the architecture and garden, ample sunlight is drawn into the interior of the room, and at the same time, casting patterns of water reflection onto the ceiling was made possible. Groundcover plants were embedded around the pond expressing a delicate detail design of plants and water adjoining.

为了方便在室内进行活动，花盆等都采用了可移动式容器。顶棚上设有一个大型天窗，这样可以使室内更加明亮。

For the functions to be held indoors, movable flower planters are used. A large skylight is cut out in the ceiling for a generous natural lighting.

涌泉用就地取材的岩石建造而成。这块岩石如同这片土地的精灵，将其放置在规划中最为重要的地方，表现对土地的敬畏之情。可爱的花朵融入周围的环境，形成了和谐的风景。

The fountain is made of a sizable stone dug out of the site. To utilize the stone in the most significant area of the site plan is a gesture in due respect to the spirit of the earth. Dainty flowers are in harmony to the surrounding area creating a natural landscape.

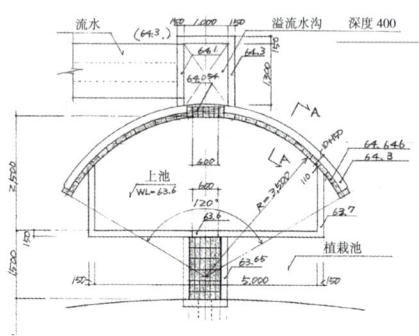

砖瓦池的平面图

全体植栽計画エスキス
Sketch of the entire landscaping plan.

总体规划系统图

借景

对于景观设计师来说，设计现场可谓聚宝盆。远近各处的风景，脚下的一棵草、一块石、一粒砂，都可以成为设计的素材。如果发现了有价值的风景，为了将其引入到设计中就需对规划用地的设计进行简化处理。不过只是这样对设计师来说还是远远不够的，设计师还需要通过空间和造型来表现出对风景的敬意。虽然可以通过景观轴的方向性或是构建框架的手法等来实现这一点，但最重要的是对借景的对象心怀敬意。

"Shakkei：borrowed scenery"

For landscape architect, construction site is a treasure island. Views of near and far distances, grass, pebbles, and sand right at the feet, everything would be element of design. If worthy scenery is found, the design of the site should be simple to incorporate the scenery. However, that is not enough for a designer. It is necessary to create homage to the scenery by expressions of space and forms. That is, expressing the direction of axis, and taking method of structuring framework, but the most significant of all is paying respect to the subject shakkei.

Tanigawa Senjuan

谷川仙寿庵
Minakami, Gunma, 2004

仙寿庵是位居全国三甲的著名高级日式旅馆。担纲建筑设计的是羽深隆雄，他将泥墙、和纸、木构件等传统工艺生动地运用到近代建筑之中。一个散发着高级日式氛围，且与周边自然环境匹配的高品质建筑空间油然而生。业主希望可以在入口处建造一个格调极高的日式庭院，以形成一个迎宾空间。第一印象对于游客十分重要。让游客在这里看见他们所期望的风景尤为关键。为了建造一个超出游客想象的高品质空间，在规划中重点推行的事项如下：

- "水之庭"，灵活运用丰富的自然水资源

源于溪涧之中的水在玄关前形成瀑布，顺流而下，汇集到位于中央的水池。不断流动的清水带来清凉顺畅的空气，形成一个清新、爽洁的空间。

- "物语庭"，配置赋有寓意的设施

仿桂离宫的大门，是景观中的一个亮点，茅草顶所蕴含的宁静氛围与后山十分匹配。相对于周围众山，尤其是谷川岳的垂直性，岩石的堆放则强调了横向性线条。脚下使用长有青苔的大型铺路石，整个景观设计给人以安定感。

- "山野之庭"，使用当地的石材和树木

铺路石以及石堆的用料均为谷川山中开采的当地石材，在一般的园林建筑工程中，通常不会使用这些石材。树木方面也选用了长期生长在当地的高大乔木，与周边宏伟的风景浑然天成，营造出山野的氛围。

Senjuan is one of the top three prominent luxury ryokan in Japan. The architecture was by Takao Habuka, and he has featured traditional craftsman work such as clay plastering, washi papers, wood joineries in the dynamic modern architecture. The architecture withhold luxurious atmosphere, harmonious with the surrounding natural environment, is of a highest quality. We were commissioned to design an entrance approach in a style of formal Japanese garden. For the arriving guests, first impression is an important factor. It is essential to be met by anticipated view. To achieve a quality beyond the expectations of the guests, the designing was processed with following key elements:

- "Water Garden" utilizing abundant natural spring water

The water drawn from the mountain cascades down a waterfall in front of the entrance, and continues to flow in a stream into the center pond. Constant flow of natural spring water draws cool freshness to the air creating refreshing garden space.

- "Story garden" of elements with significances

The gate, a focal element, is designed as homage to the Katsura Detached Palace, and its subdued thatched roof matches well with the mountains in the backdrop. The stone arrangements emphasize horizontal line against the verticality of the nearby mountains, notably the peaks of Tanigawa. Moss covered wide stepping-stones were used for paving, and a garden with stable image was achieved in totality.

- "Mountain village garden" making use of local stones and trees

The stones for the paving and arrangements were quarried from the local mountains of Tanigawa. Many of the type of stones normally not used in gardens were employed. Large local aged trees were brought in to create an atmosphere of a mountain village that fuses into the dynamic landscape of the area.

对面页：庭园入口处的门，引用了日本第一名园桂离宫的门。

正门入口处的园路引导人们走向位于左手边靠里的玄关，斜着指向建筑物，通过这种设计来提高人们在前进时的期待感。园路两侧种植的乔木绿荫深邃，作为视线的聚焦点，与后方的大山形成了一种绝妙的匀称感。

The approach path leading diagonally towards the building in the left hand corner is devised to heighten anticipation as taking steps closer. In creating a sense of depth, tall trees are planted on either side of the path and in the backdrop lies the mountains in exquisite visual balance.

越过建筑的屋顶，可看见"谷川岳"的白雪。

在仙寿庵之中最具有魅力的，就是后方谷川岳的雪景。从大门一进入庭院，就能透过近景落叶树看见谷川岳的雪景，加深并渲染了人们到达目的地的印象。在垂直的景观中加入丰富的庭园要素而构成的风景，是这里的特色。

The most attractive feature of Senjuan is the snow-covered view of the Mt. Tanigawa. Entering through the gate, it appears through the deciduous trees in the foreground presenting a striking impression to the arriving guests. The characteristic feature of this garden is the composition by building up of various elements to the verticality of the landscape.

小假山、横卧的大石块、水流与瀑布共同构成了玄关的正面景观。石头未做堆砌，单独地摆放在此，为的是充分显现石块的形状和奇特的质感。尤其是下方的瀑布石，特意选用了受水流侵蚀而造型独特之物，丰富景观的变化。水流大弯度地蜿蜒流淌，展现出柔美的质感。

The composition in front of the main entrance is a small artificial hill, a large laid stone, water canal, and a waterfall. To feature the shapes and characters of the stones having qualities of their own, they were used separately rather than arranging in groups. Especially, the stones placed in the lower end of the waterfall having features eroded in the river, add interest to the scenery. The stream curves in a smooth ample sweeping line, expressing a soothing ambience.

通透的竹篱（光悦寺篱）与其背后隐藏的土墙共同标示庭院的范围。主庭在竹篱深处，若隐若现；匀称的枝叶映照在土墙上，树影婆娑。水边的草坪缓缓延展，氛围平和，点缀用水钵和堆石，令空间更有亲切感。

The see-through bamboo fence (Kouetsu-ji fence) and the mud wall indicate garden boundary. The main garden beyond the bamboo fence is partially visible here and there, and just enough branches of the trees softly silhouette against the mud wall. Gradual slope of lawn spread along the edge of water; otherwise a mellow atmosphere is accentuated with stone arrangement and basin.

将人们的视线引向庭院外的水流和轻柔地划分出庭院内外领域的竹篱，勾画出庭院深深的画面。岩石顺其自然地卧放着，直线性的排列营造了深远的景色。

The canal leading the eyes beyond and the oblique boundary of the bamboo fence emphasize the depth of the garden. By unpretentiously laying the stones low, and arranging in a straight line, a profound landscape is achieved.

庭院中的石头卧放着，并且呈相互对视状。卧石连接着紧在其后的竹与土两种不同素材的墙体，与墙上映照的树影一起烘托出一种柔和的氛围。

In this garden, the stones are laid low in symmetrical relation. The fences of different materials of mud and bamboo are connected with the crouching stone in the foreground, and along with the silhouette of the branches, a gentle ambience is expressed.

对于日本庭园来说，水流是一个不可或缺的要素。尤其是逆光而见的水面，其变化和闪烁的波光十分美丽，再加上阳光透过落叶树（枫树）的红叶照射在庭园之中，将庭园丰富的景观展现在人们的面前。树叶的影子映在地衣上，与落叶共谱季节的篇章。

In Japanese gardens, water element plays an important role. Especially, the radiance and transitions of water surface glistening in backlight is breathtakingly beautiful, and the sunlight streaming through the maple leaves adds richness to the expressions of the garden. Tree shadows over the moss with the autumn foliage together contributes seasonal effect.

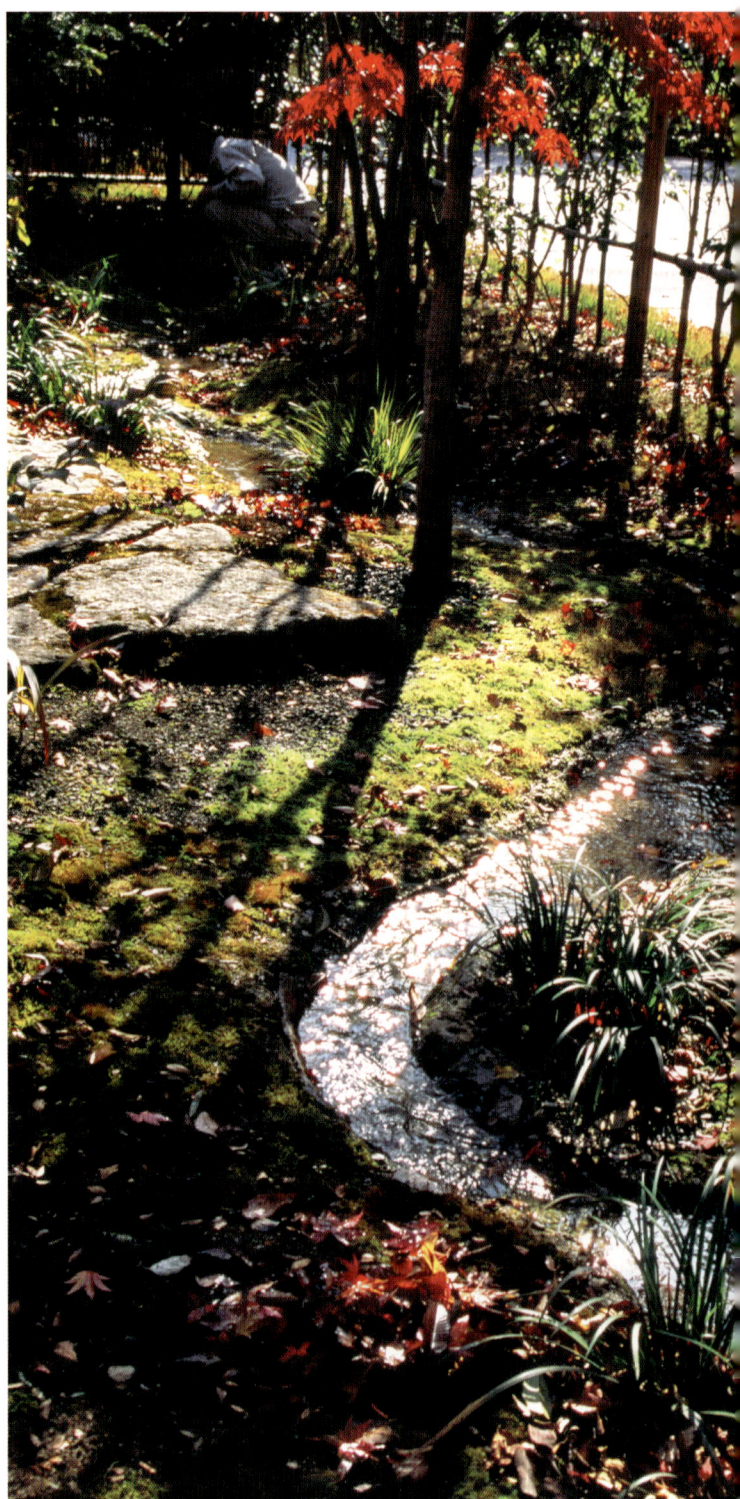

风土

为了暂时远离日常生活，我们会去旅行。虽然目的各不相同，但是住宿场所在很大程度上左右我们对旅行的印象。谋求基本的便利性自是不在话下，而能够享受一种绝无仅有的体验，才是人们在旅行中真正的追求所在。因此，接待方除了要准备最好的设施之外，还需要以个性丰富的陈设来款待游客。这指的是什么呢？这是指：以当地的风土为背景，向人们提供充裕的服务空间。自古就存在于这片土地上的事物与这里的空气相融合，尤其是植物，自然地生长着，原有的美丽留存至今。正是这种宁静的风情，舒缓了游客的心灵。

Cultural climate

We go away on trips to temporarily escape from our daily routine life. The reasons for traveling may vary, but place of sojourn definitely makes a difference in the impression of the trip. Moreover the basic accommodations, it is for the experience that can only be attained at the destination is often the drive to travel. Therefore, the host must show hospitality offering utmost accommodation and entertain with distinctive furnishings. Namely, it is the richness of servicing space supported by local culture and climate. What has existed locally for length of time is natural in its local climate. Vegetation, especially, will grow free of strain and sustain its attractive natural features. It is such refinement that solaces the travelers.

Yume No Shima Tropical Botanical Garden

梦之岛热带植物馆
Yumenoshima, Tokyo,　1987

　　东京是从古时江户时代开始，以填海造陆的方式扩大生活空间形成的都市。20世纪后期，都市的废弃物被大量用作填埋材料。当时新建的"梦之岛"虽以如此美丽的名字命名，原本却是一个20世纪堆积废弃物的"垃圾岛"。临近小岛的地方设有垃圾焚烧处理装置。20世纪80年代后期，开始推行利用垃圾焚烧产生的热源建立温室的规划。

　　温室向来都是环境、园艺教学的场所，多作为活教材加以使用，常展示热带花草、供人赏花。而本项目重点突出"空间戏剧"的特征，规划创建充满娱乐气氛的空间。

　　设计的灵感来源于传统日本庭园，使用池泉环游式庭园系统的做法。该系统主要利用水景，通过设置"流水"和"池泉"营造景观区，顺水徒步前行，一路可以欣赏到所有重要的节点，步移景异，景色一气呵成。单行路线始于一层的入口处，让游客们体味完各种精彩场景后，最终到达二层的出口。入口设置在瀑布的正面，顺着延伸至水边的曲线斜坡一路而下，然后从瀑布水帘后穿行而过。池中种植着王莲等珍贵而独具风采的水生植物。透过瀑布的水帘回望水池与入口处的风景，然后再缓缓地登上斜坡，穿过隧道，来到温室的中心。用椰树叶盖顶搭建的独具异国风情的小亭子，为游客们提供了歇息的场所。小亭的后方设置了一个小丘，游客们在小亭中停留休息的同时，还能聆听瀑布声与潺潺的流水声。沿着更加弯曲的庭园小径前行到小木桥，可以看到下方的第二个水池与茶室。顶部与二层同高，在此设置了小小的空间，可以让游客们在游园的最后稍作停留并回望走过的庭园小径。

Dating back as Edo period, Tokyo is a city having expanded its habitation land by reclaiming the sea. In the late 20th century, most of the reclamation source was the immense amount of disposed waste from the urban area. Yume No Shima (Dream Island), in contrary to the name, was a new but filthy waste deposited product of the 20th century. On the adjacent land was an incinerator facility, and in the late 1980s, the tropical greenhouse project utilizing its heat source was launched.

Generally, botanical gardens were planned as an educational institution for environment and horticulture studies where rare tropical plants are displayed and was merely appreciating the flowers. Therefore, this greenhouse project aimed to create a space for dramatic experiences with an air of entertainment quality.

The clue to the idea came from Japanese gardens and was planned to adopt the chisen-kaiyu-shiki (wet strolling) garden system. The system was utilizing water elements as streams and fountains to create focal points so that the visitors as they follow the promenade are able to experience all of the attractions in a sequence of a brush stroke. From the entrance on the ground level, the one-way pedestrian promenade leads through various points of interest to the exit on the upper level. At the entrance visitors will face the main focal point of a waterfall and guided by curving slope down to the waterside and behind the waterfall. In the pond, impressive and unique plants as Victoria amazonica are cultivated. From behind the waterfall the pond and entrance area are observed, and in a gradual climbing slope continues through the tunnel. Where is approximately the center of the greenhouse, an exotic gazebo with a palm thatched roof is placed as a resting place. Nestled against a hill, visitors can rest listening to the refreshing sound of the waterfall running into the stream. From there, the path takes a further winding route and from the wooden bridge, the second pond and a refreshment area can be overlooked. At the top of the level, there is a small landing for the purpose of looking back over the route.

对面页：进入后的首处胜景——瀑布，穿过瀑布背后的小路进入温室内部。

孩子们愉快地走在水帘中，精神
饱满地准备出发去温室探险。

The excited children are walking
through the trail behind the water.
Their lively figures going off to the
garden expedition is doubled with an
image of their future.

世界著名的温室都在上空保留了
巨大的空间。该温室是由一个最
高36米的中央圆顶以及与之相称
的两个圆形屋顶构成，为种植棕
榈类提供了条件。棕榈类植物的
垂直感是温室的重要景观元素，
它那清爽直立的身姿扣动着观赏
者的心弦，让人们真切地感受阳
光为植物的生长给予恩惠的瞬间。

The notable greenhouses in the
world are determined by whether
a large void is secured. This
greenhouse consists of a central
dome ceiling having a height of
36m at the highest point, and two
other domes accordingly, providing
for the growth of palm trees.
Verticality of the palm trees is an
important landscape element of the
greenhouse, and the cool refreshing
figures of the trees are striking. It is also
in such moments to become aware
that the blessing of the sun directly
contributes to survival of life.

山中的水池上架着高高的木桥，细细的瀑布下落的水声如同在幽谷中回荡似的萦绕在耳边。正面的桥下设计一些小瀑布，演绎着多变而深幽的景象。

Over the pond in the mountain, a tall wooden bridge is hung, and the sound of falling water from the narrow cascade echoes pleasantly against the deep topography. There is also a low waterfall below the front bridge for visual diversity and effect for the depth in the space.

温室中还为到此一游的人们设置了餐厅，在这里可以欣赏宽敞舒适的风景。为游客提供一个空间，使他们能有时间悠闲地从不同的角度再次观赏、回味看过的景色，这在景观设计中尤为重要。

The restaurant entertains the visitors returning from the tour with a relaxing view. It is essential in landscape design to offer a space and time to enjoy looking over the scenery from another angle.

小亭的顶棚是用菲律宾引进的棕榈叶铺盖而成的，颇具南洋群岛的素朴风情。每天这里都会进行几次模拟夏日骤雨的大面积洒水，坐在小亭中聆听雨滴落在椰树叶上的声音，仿佛让人忘却身处日本。

The roof of the gazebo is thatched with palm leaves imported from the Philippines for an unaffected tropical atmosphere. Several times a day, a rain shower like sprinkler waters the entire greenhouse, and listening to the sound of raindrops hitting the palm leaves in the gazebo, it makes you forget you are in Japan.

凉亭

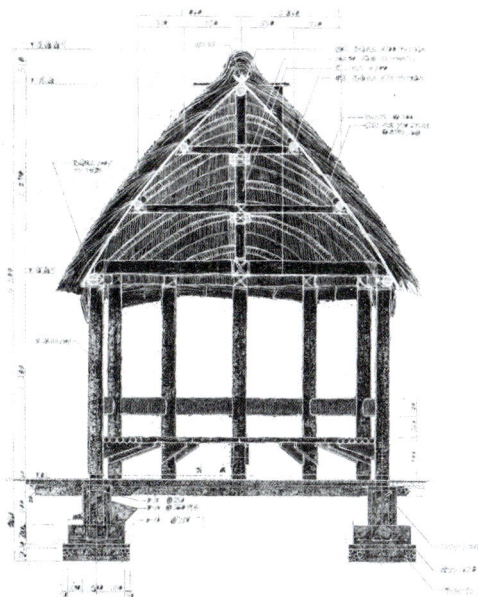

在铺满绿叶花草的庭园小径看到隧道，给人们增添些许惊险感。幼童紧握母亲的手的身影惹人怜爱。

"A dark tunnel a midst lots of greens and flowers makes me nervous." A child holding tightly onto mother's hand is adorable.

温室内多姿多彩、奇特有趣。

脑内的观光休闲

进入主题公园还需要进行精神上的准备。为即将欣赏体验的空间做好心理准备，调整好自己的心情让自己彻底融入角色，这样才能体味无穷的乐趣。在这个热带植物园中，游客们只需看到并体验自己喜欢的景色就可以了。毕竟主题公园无法达到真正的完美，而想要达到"完美"的迪斯尼乐园，会有些让人气喘吁吁的感觉。游客们只需将欣赏过的景色在大脑中重演，作为第二次观光休闲的体验，这样就能获得自己理想的空间与时间。而所谓的主题公园，就是为游客们创造这样机会的场所。

A resort in the brain

To enter into a theme park, a mental preparation is a necessity. Unless you are prepared to "act out" the experience you will be going through, the enjoyment of it will be lost. In this tropical botanical garden, you are free to enjoy whatever that pleases you. It is because there are no perfect theme parks. Disneyland aimed to be a perfect park is somehow feels suffocating. If the participants could recreate the vision of their experience into a resort experience in their mind, an ideal personal space and time will be created. Theme parks may be considered as the device for such creation.

公 园 景 观
Landscape Design of Park

　　日本的城市公园依法而建，公园的布置设施安装也都要按规行事，个性设计很少。虽说对公园进行过多的设计会影响公园平静的氛围，但就现状来看，相当多的公园显得毫无生趣。在此将向大家介绍三个有特色的公园，分别是供儿童游玩的小公园；自然树林和池塘相连、地形起伏的公园；以及平地上可供人们聚集、拥有都市规模的广场和户外音乐厅的公园。

　　每个公园的周边环境和功能虽各不相同，但都贯穿一个共同的主题，那就是公园在一个整体设计的故事性以及各自细节的多变性层面上，为来访的人们提供美妙多彩的时光。

　　The codes pertaining to urban parks are provided in Japan, and oftentimes standards are drawn as to the facility contents and layout inhibiting innovative designs. It is not necessary for each park to be characteristic, but it is a fact that many uninteresting parks exist. In these pages are introduced three parks; a small park where many children play, a park with undulated geography connecting natural forest and pond, and another park consisting of urban scale plaza and an outdoor music hall.

　　Although each park has different surrounding environment and functions, there is a common theme where enriched time to users is provided by narrative in entirety or in details, and/or abundance in diversity of detail design.

道路驿站"天童温泉"

大沼一丁目公园

鹤川真光寺公园

Road Station "Tendo Onsen"

道路驿站 "天童温泉"
Tendo, Yamagata, 2004

本次景观设计的目的是突显 "出羽的三森"，通过眺望奥羽山脉、月山、鸟海山达到维护空间特性的目的，与此同时，让人们重新认识孕育风土的地域景观也是要达到的目的之一。对于需配备功能的广阔空间，通过 "间隔空间"、"非规律性"、"摇曳" 等多种平衡性操作手法，对地形、绿化植栽以及设施进行设置，创造出空间的深邃感与适度的距离感。同时通过具有舒缓的水平延伸性的地面设计，利用其与线条明晰的针叶树以及照明装置的对比，在空间上形成竖向的对比。

站在项目用地远眺群山，自身宛如是大自然的一部分。随着视线跨越用地，融入远处的山与天之间。近景与中景处的设计空间和作为背景的群山形成 "地" 与 "图" 的关系。"地" 与 "图" 的连续与重复，带来令人屏息的延伸感与空间的开阔感。

这个项目对于景观设计师而言，不仅可以进行室外空间的设计，更是有幸能够参与室外舞台等建筑方面的设计。考虑到日常的需要以及天气因素，采用可以负荷积雪重量的膜结构屋顶，确保了屋檐下的采光度。背面的移动式窗帘设计为可伸缩，通过故意忽略对足下部分的设计，实现多功能广场与草坪广场在空间上的连续性。为避免屋顶膜层因积雪而弯曲变形，采用了 A 型悬架构造膜，屋顶的龙骨架构隐藏在膜结构之下。采用施加张力的环形结构形成两个细圆锥形顶盖，隐喻当地天童传说中，降临舞鹤山的两位童子和他们的衣裳。

为满足多种多样的活动需求，在多功能广场上配置了三种采用耐负荷钢格板制的喷泉，增强举办活动和日常使用时在舒适度上的需求。夜间，喷泉还能作为照明柱，勾画如梦幻般的美丽空间。该用地已成为市民引以为豪的公共空间，是开展各种纪念日活动及举办庆典的重要场所。

Enhancement of the Dewa no Mitsumori, referring to the three representative mountains of the old Dewa province, and integrating the Ou Mountain Range, Mt. Gassan, and Mt. Chokaisan into the view was the solution to create identity of the site. Functionally required wide open space was composed balancing out unconventional break offs and spacing to the topography, greenery, and facilities for depths and intervals, and applying sharp vertical lines of facility elements and evergreen trees to the horizontal stretch of space.

Standing here looking at the mountains in yonder, it feels as if your own body fuse into nature and become a part of it. It is the effect of landscapes of forefront, mid-range and the mountains interacting the relation of "ground" and "figure" in multifold where overwhelming depth and sense of expansion is produced.

As a landscape architect, we were given an opportunity to design the open theater along with planning of outdoor space. In consideration of the daily use, a roof is of weight withstanding membrane structure for ability to secure ample daylight. Collapsible curtain in the rear, made possible to be stored away, has openings at the foot to create a sense of continuation with the multi-purpose plaza and the lawn. Type-A membrane suspension structure was adopted for the roof for the strength against the heavy weight of snow, and hid the structures appearing through the roofing screen. The two suspensions created by the pull of the rings is a metaphor to the Tendo legend of the child gods and their robes descended to Mt. Maitsuru.

The multi-purpose plaza consists of three variations of water fountains installed with weight proof gratings, coping with special functions and daily amenity. In the evenings, the fountains are turned into pillars of light producing magical ambience. The plaza, having become the pride of the citizens, are now intensively used as the main venue of festivals and functions.

对面页：与背景群山形成对比、直指蓝天的室外舞台。

相对于周围线条柔和的山脉，入口空间采用肃穆感的垂直性设计，整个空间显得大气而富有韵律。

The approach was designed applying vertical lines in contrast to the gentle skyline of the mountain range for a dynamic rhythmical landscape.

道路驿站"天童温泉"总平面图

比例 1:1000

表现背景处山与广场关系的手绘图

石片堆积的景墙清晰地勾
画出草坪，山与舞台的轮
廓，渲染水平线的存在感
让人意识到延伸至山中轴线作用的石凳

与游玩器具相结合的地形

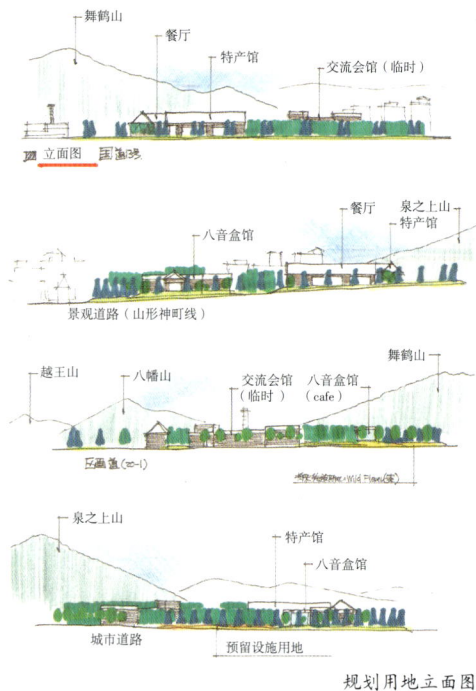

規劃用地立面圖

进入仿佛被群山包围的规划用地，总会让人产生与远处的风景化为一体的感觉。周边配置柔和的植物，使景色与外围的山脉更为融合。

Stepping into the site nestled in the surrounding mountains, one would be overtaken by a sense of fusion with the far landscape. With delicate arrangement of the trees, an intimate relation to the mountains is produced.

采用天然石等作为素材，让人们能更好地感受自然。由于阳光照射角度不同，石材表面产生有趣的反射，展现了独特的质感。

Natural stones were applied for the effect of naturalness, and the attractive uniqueness of material quality is expressed with the transition of the sunlight reflection.

广场边界具有长凳功能的堆石、铺装图样。

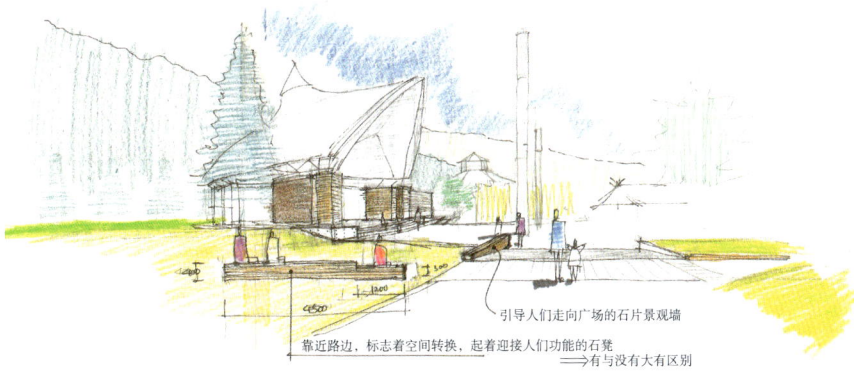

室外舞台周边的手绘图

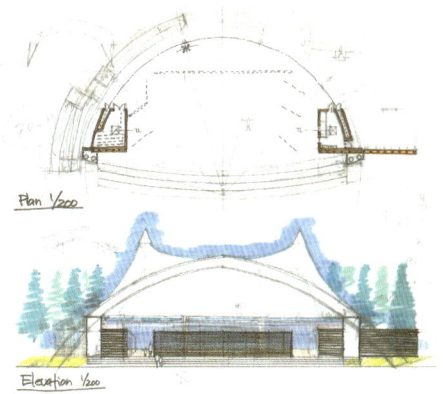

室外舞台平面图、立面图

室外舞台中指向蓝天的两个锥形顶盖表现两位童子纯洁的身姿。作为标志性设施的同时还具有多种使用功能。

The double peaks of the roof of the outdoor theater projecting into the sky symbolize the legendary child gods descended from heaven. As the representative facility of the site, the theater adapts to diverse functional needs.

草坡上玩耍的孩子与母亲

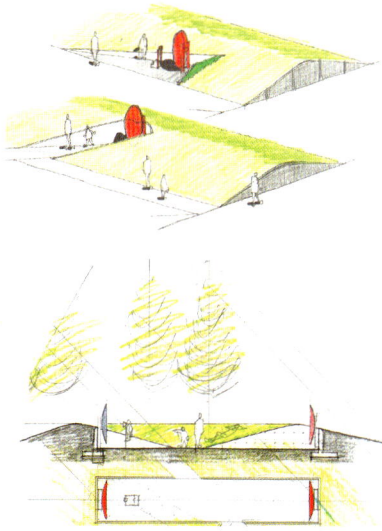

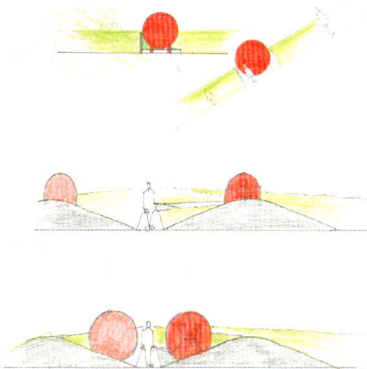

产生回声的游玩器具

展现各种水的表情，奇趣的儿童游乐景观。

夜幕临近，广场上满是望着喷泉、脸上洋溢着幸福的人们。夕阳照耀下的他们，或许正与家人聊着今天的趣事吧。

As the dusk sets in, faces of people looking at the fountains show expression of content. With faces glowing in the setting sun, families may be talking to each other about how the day was.

喷泉及戏水儿童

夕阳斜照的广场中悠然自得的人们

地与图

要达到尽显空间美丽的目的，必须有效地处理并应用好"地"与"图"的关系。就如春日的樱花（视作"图"），在绿意盎然的树林衬托之下，会显得更加美丽灿烂。本次规划以广场中心处遥望所见到的群山为"地"，以眼前的各种广场设施为"图"来进行布局。从一直存在的植物和景观小品，到瞬间出现的喷泉，这些丰富变化的景色，借助背景的映衬，成为宣示存在感的美丽空间。

Ground and Figure

For esthetic quality of space, it is necessary to use the relation of "ground" and "figure" effectively. When set against a dark green forest, cherry blossoms of spring will be further enhanced. In this project, "ground" is the mountains in the background, and various facilities arranged in the foreground are the "figure." From the stable trees and furniture to the sudden appearance of water fountain, the scenery transitions supported by the backdrop landscape exists as a beautiful space.

Onuma I-Chome Park

大沼一丁目公园
Kodaira, Tokyo, 2002

街区公园的规模一般都较小，并且必须满足一些标准的基本功能，因此在设计时往往只是对既定的设施、设备进行布置，而鲜少有个性化的作品。相对而言，大沼一丁目公园的规模比较大，在设计上就具有较大的自由发挥度。公园位于公共住宅密集的区域，针对会有众多居民光顾这一点，提出了与普通街区公园大相径庭、独具特色的公园设计方案。设计主题是多种多样的"玩"。整个公园划分为四个区域，使公园的游戏空间能够适应不同年龄层的孩子们的游戏方式，从而满足居住在周边的众多孩子们的多种需求。

我们将原有的大樱花树纳入西部的区域，并采用格子状的铺装，布置代表公园风格的广场，表现出次序井然之感。在硬质铺装的广场内，孩子们创造自己的娱乐空间，进行溜冰等活动。

水的景点是由涌水口流出的喷泉和流水以及小水池构成。孩子们在形式变换着的水中发现各种玩耍的方式，展现他们活泼的身姿。

安置游乐设施的广场则以游乐设施为基础开展多种游戏，运动场则成为高年级学生们进行球类竞技的场所。

虽然在起伏的草地空间中没有什么新颖的玩耍方式，但相信孩子们一定能发挥他们的想像力，去做各种有趣的游戏。

环顾这四个区域，可以看到孩子随着年龄的增长，游戏的方式也会从固定的游乐设施逐步转向自己花工夫去发现并创造新的游戏。从这个项目中学到的极为重要的一点就是：根据孩子们的成长，创出有多样选择的玩耍空间。

There are not many characteristic urban parks exist due to the fact the sites are small, normally, and are mere application of standardized formats. Where as, this Onuma 1-chome Park have a fairly large area enabling some ingenuity. Located within a public housing site where many people will be taking advantage, a park with a characteristic quality was proposed. The concept is various type of "play." The site was divided into four general zones to suit different generation groups of children.

To begin with, the western zone is composed featuring orderliness as the representative area of the park with grid pattern paving enclosing existing large cherry tree. Children seem to have discovered on own an ideal location for roller-skating, etc.

The water zone consists of a spouting fountain, water channel, and a pond. Responding to the various expressions of water elements, activities are initiated and sprightly children are observed.

Where the playground equipments are fixed, equipment based games are generated, and in the sports field, older children indulge in ball games.

In the undulated lawn area, no innovative activities are seen yet, but there is no doubt, children will find something eventually.

Looking over the four zones, it could be observed that children as they get older, grow out of fixed equipments and start developing games of their own devise. This was a project enabled us to become aware of the importance of allowing wide flexibilities adapting to the growth of children.

对面页：公园的设施既保护现有树林又可增添乐趣。
在直线构成的空间中配置流水、池、花架、凳椅、
游玩器具。

为后部住宅区修建的公园中，保存了原有栽种大樱花树的草坡。

供嬉水用的椭圆形水池，用花架和凳椅等迎接了成年人。

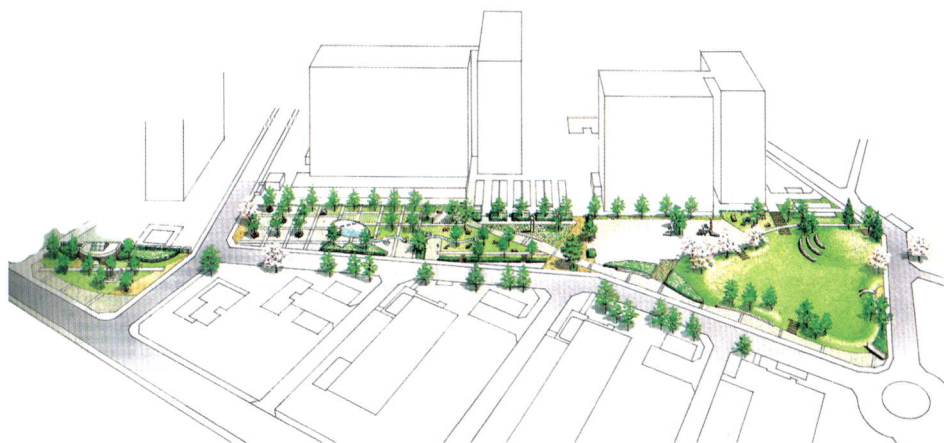

划分为格子状的区域内安装着具有各
种功能的游乐设施，通过流水与小池
连接。在直线中添加有机的线条，不
仅赋予空间流动性，还拉近了与孩子
们活动的关联性。

Diverse play equipments dot through the
area divided in grids and are connected
by water channel and pond. By applying
organic patterns into straight formal
lines produces fluidity in the space, and
relativity to the activities of the children
are further enhanced.

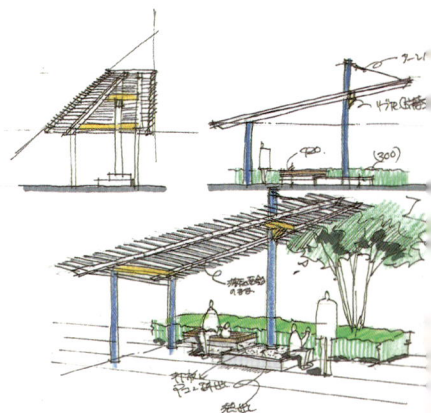

花架效果图

广场中需要能够驻足的地方，如果配上可以让人休息的设施则更好。用花架遮阳，为那些在池中戏水的孩子们提供休息场所。

In open wide spaces, a shelter is necessary, and even better if it could be a facility to rest. A pergola intercepting the summer sun is a place for the children at the swimming pool to refuge.

将原有的樱花树纳入格状空间，大树用浓密的枝叶宣示了自身的空间领域，整个景观由此更具深度。

The existing cherry tree enclosed in a grid paving extends its boundary with its outstretched branches creating a depth in the landscape.

游乐设施以黄色为基调，渲染明亮感。

功能

作为城市的配套设施，公园需要实现各种功能。如本设计中的小空间，也需要设置老幼皆宜、动静兼备的空间。规划者会将"必要"的功能以及设施纳入设计范围，然而仅仅这么做还远远不够。不仅要讲究设计的质量，更要为整个空间或部分区域创造故事。使用者不会仅仅满足于只是将功能罗列出来的公园，他们需要的是更为丰富多彩的空间与时光。

Function

Parks are required of various functions as an urban facility. Even in a limited space as this project, both active and passive space designs are required to cope to the needs of groups of all ages, from the young and to old. A designer will incorporate the "necessary" functions and facilities into the plan, but that is never "sufficient." Needless to say a quality of design, but stories or narratives must be contrived in parts and whole of the park. The users will never be satisfied with a mere enumeration of functions, but expect enriched space and time at the place.

看到孩子们活泼玩耍的身姿总是令人心情愉快。根据不同年龄层与性别，设计不同的场所及设备以供使用。希望这个公园能为人们留下孩童时的美好记忆。

It is delightful to watch children enjoying themselves. Choices of space and equipments are prepared to cope with children's ages and gender. We hope the park will be remembered as a venue of happy memories of childhood days.

公园的主角是孩子，欢叫与来回奔跑的身影中映射对未来的希望。

游玩器具及嬉戏的孩子们

Tsurukawa Shinkoji Park

鹤川真光寺公园
Machida, Tokyo, 1997

鹤川台新城的规划理念是：保存原有斜面缓坡绿地，创造新的绿地并推进绿地的网络化进程，营建符合居住新城的公园，构成精巧、细腻的空间。新城的地形由西向东呈缓坡状下降，而真光寺公园则位于西部的最高处。与新城同时对外开放的公园，作为人与自然共生的街区中的标志性空间场所，为人们提供了各种各样的设施，引导游园者们在此开展多样的活动。

- 将缓坡绿地引入公园，并设置收集雨水的景池。
- 设置大气、有力度感的草坡，作为俯视街区的"记忆之丘"。
- 巧妙地设置四个造型各异的凉亭（眺望之家、谷之家、街区之家、水之家），为长时间逗留的游人提供休息的场所。
- 不仅有放置游乐设施的广场，还设置了"野地"等，供人们自由地进行各类活动。
- 设置停车场以及管理楼，为游园者提供服务。

上述空间虽然结构简洁地配置在公园中，但通过地形的高低起伏、蜿蜒的庭园小径以及配种的植栽，让园中的设施若隐若现，呈现一幅深幽且连续多彩的景色。

与此同时，以斜面缓坡的自然林，表现了"绿"这一景观设计中的基本要素；以园内汇集雨水的景池表现了"水"的要素；以生机盎然的缓坡草坪表现了"大地"的要素。通过这些要素展现自然开阔的景观。

The concept of Tsurukawadai New Town planning was to conserve the existing afforested slope, forming new green tract to blend, and in consideration as a residential district, a garden like landscape was carefully planned. The New Town site is on a gentle slope running from west to east, and the Shinkoji Park locates on the highest point in the western area. The park that opened to the public simultaneously with the inauguration of the town symbolizes the theme of symbiotic existing of people and nature provides various facilities for community activities.

The natural green slope is incorporated into the park, and a scenic rainwater pond was created.

A dynamic grass hill overlooking the town as "Hill of Memories" was formed.

Four differently themed and shaped gazebos, "House of Scenic View," "House of Valley," "House of Town," and "House of Water" were tactfully placed providing for lengthy stays.

Besides the amusement area for children, playgrounds as wide grassy lawns to be freely enjoyment are provided.

As a service to the visitors, parking space and an administration office was established.

Although the composition is of a simple layout, the undulation of the ground level, the curving of the promenade, and planting of the trees, visual depths and sequence variation of the landscape are contrived. The basic design element of "greenery" provided by the natural forest of the slope, "water" by the scenic rainwater pond, and "earth" by the dynamic grassy slope together express a rich landscape.

对面页：草坪广场北端的凉亭，林中舒畅的休息场所。

抽空登上小山丘，眺望一下自己生活的城市风景，可谓是一种幸福。家人与朋友们所在的街区自身就是充满爱意的景观。为达到这样的效果，自然地将这个俯视街区全貌的公园勾绘成高品位、简洁而美丽的空间。

"Occasionally, I climb up the hill over our town and enjoy the view. I feel content. The town where my family and friends live has a lovely landscape. Of course, the park at the foot of the hill should be simple, of high quality, and beautiful."

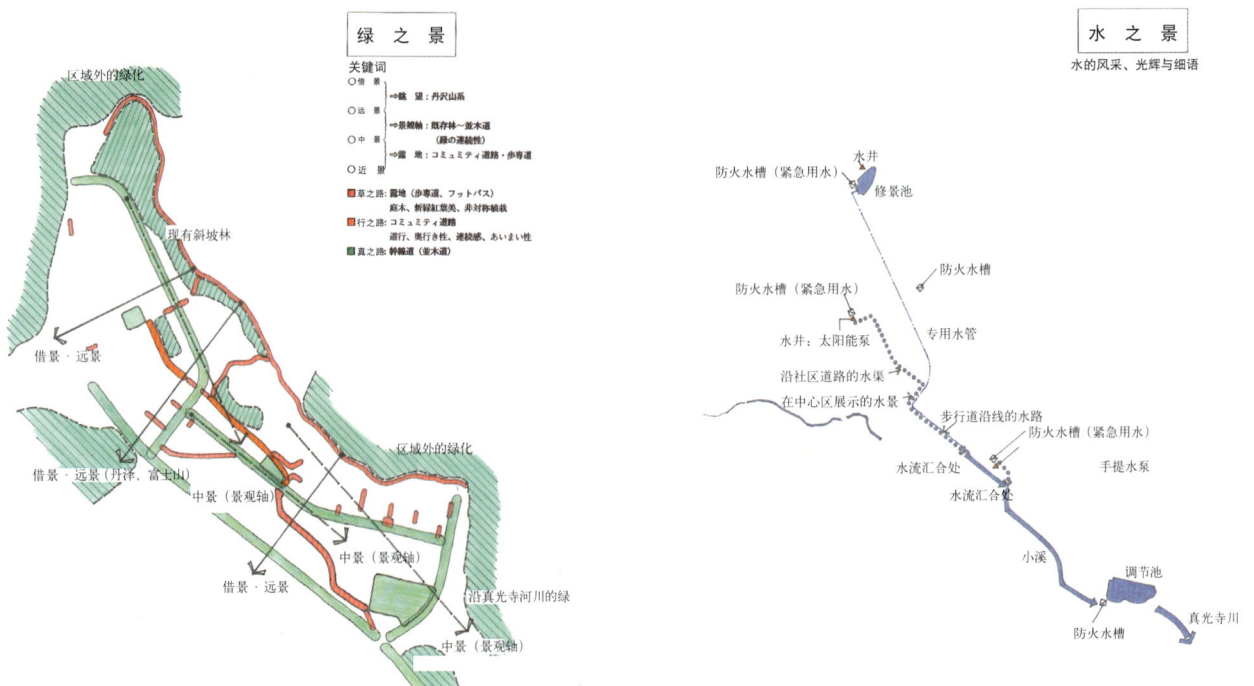

绿 之 景

关键词

○借 景 ⇒眺 望：丹沢山系

○远 景 ⇒景观轴：既存林～並木道
（緑の連続性）

○中 景 ⇒露 地：コミュニティ道路・步專道

○近 景

■草之路：露地（步專道、フットパス）
庭木、斬綠紅葉美、井对称轴载

■行之路：コミュニティ道路
遊行、奧行き性、连续感、あいまい性

■真之路：幹線道（並木道）

区域外的绿化

现有斜坡林

借景·远景

借景·远景（丹泽、富士山）

中景（景观轴）

中景（景观轴）

借景·远景

沿真光寺河川的绿

中景（景观轴）

区域外的绿化

水 之 景

水的风采、光辉与细语

防火水槽（紧急用水）

水井

修景池

防火水槽

防火水槽（紧急用水）

水井：太阳能泵

专用水管

沿社区道路的水渠

在中心区展示的水景

步行道沿线的水路

防火水槽（紧急用水）

水流汇合处

手提水泵

水流汇合处

小溪

调节池

防火水槽

真光寺川

110 — Landscape Design of Park

公园小品在看与被看之间成为景观。缓坡上的凉亭，位于广场上两个景观构筑物正中间的轴线上。

A landscape is sustained by a mutual relation of the park elements to be looked at and users to look. The belvedere situated on a gradual mound is in a midpoint of the axis line between the twin monuments.

平缓的草坪撩动游客的心，引导着人们的行为举动。倾斜度略大的草坪上部人们卧躺着休息，下部则是孩子在愉快地玩耍。

Gentle sloping lawn is alluring to the visitors as it is, and leads the way. People lying on the grass where the slope is a little steeper and at the lower area children playing can be observed.

游乐设施宽松地置放在宽敞的空间里，器具的色调缓和，与周围的色彩互相协调，并与木制的百叶一起，营造出高品质的游憩景观空间。

The play equipments are arranged spaciously. The tone-downed colors matching the surrounding area, together with the wooden louver fence, a high quality space is achieved.

概念效果图

入口的景观构筑物采用锐角设计，与周边柔和的自然景观形成鲜明对比。来访者在两座景观构筑物中间停放自行车，演示人们在广阔空间中需要寻得一些倚靠物的心理特征。

The twin monuments at the gate with sharp design are made to contrast against the softness of the natural surrounding. People leaving their bicycles in between the monuments is a good psychological case study of the need of an refuge in a open wide space.

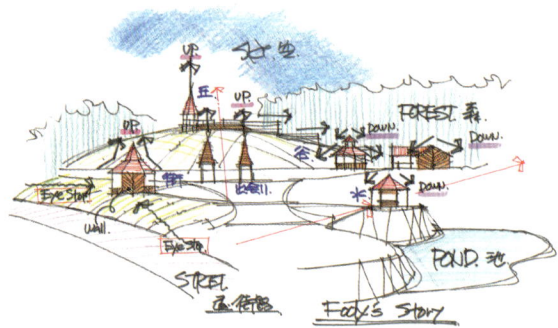

面向小丘凉亭的阶梯使用木制材料，勾画出柔和的曲线。随着草坪不断地延伸，与小丘连为一体，成为一种铺装纹样。

The wooden steps leading to the belvedere draws a gentle curving line. The grass will eventually cover the steps and integrate the steps into the texture of the hill.

采用二重顶棚的凉亭独具存在感，为周边景色增添了变化。曲线的庭园小径、斜坡的量感、若隐若现的景观构筑物，所有的风景素材在景观中发挥了重要作用。

The existence of the two-tiered belvedere gives the landscape diverse appearances. Winding promenade, volume of the slope, and glimpse of the twin monument are all significant elements of the landscape.

宽阔的草坪与其背后的自然林相互映衬、形成风景，给人一种通透、清爽的感觉。草坪为"地"，自然林、凉亭、游园的人们是"图"，展现多姿的景色。

Compatibility as scenery is good, and I feel freshness with ··· wildwood in respect and the back of a wide lawn.. scenery. The lawn side becomes "Ground", the natural forest, pavilion and the people in the park become "Figure", and scenery with the change is offered to us.

规划平面图

SCALE=1:1000

将公园中不经意的一角作为登上小丘的入口，对其进行精巧细腻的设计。人们对细部空间的综合体验形成对风景的印象，因此细部空间的设计极其重要。

It is assumed a fine design as an entrance climbs hill though it is a corner with a nonchalant park. Because the person has the impression of scenery as the whole of the accumulation of a detailed space, the design of small space is really important.

小丘上的凉亭设计为向天鼎立的形态，底部则由木板铺装形成一个广场，使之成为一个舒适的空间。

The pergola from which it stands on the hill is assumed to be a design postponed with heavenward, and Adachi secures the plaza with a wooden deck, and assumes a comfortable space.

秋日，四周的红叶环抱公园，展现出一幅与夏日完全不同的柔和景象。人们在野外休闲娱乐的同时，还能在此尽享秋日充裕的风情。

In fall, the park will be enveloped in autumn foliage. In the softer sunlight than that of the summer, people enjoy in their activities. This is an ideal place to relish the richness of autumn season.

秋日里，夏天无法看到的树木的细微变化得以呈现。红叶、落叶为树木带来更多变幻，与游园者的活动相映衬，展现更为意味深幽的景象。

The slight differences of the forest become noticeable in autumn. Colored leaves, fallen leaves, change appearances of the trees and along with the activities of people, profound scenery develops.

眺望

看与被看如同表里，是一体。古日式庭园的最精彩处是山顶，在拥有登至峰顶的成就感的同时，可以俯视周围的场所。此外，日式庭院设计中时有"回望"这一关键词存在。每到达一个节点，回望来路，并在焦点处设置标志物。

处于观看方的景物，也肯定会成为被看的一方。在回游路线上重复"看"与"被看"这两个视角相互转换的关系，将连续性景观不断向前推进，为游园者带来多重乐趣。

Prospect

To look and looked at are always two side of a coin. It is also so for historic Japanese gardens, climax is at the top of the landscape, a place for sense of accomplishment, and at the same time, to prospect the view. Furthermore, various prospecting points are dotted along the path called mikaeri, to look back, and a landmark is set in the point of focus.

To be standing at a point of prospecting would be standing at a prospected point in reverse. The sequence of repetition of this prospecting and prospected relation through the stroll is a multilayered enjoyment.

校 园 景 观

Landscape Design of Campus

　　日本自古以来把学校形容为"学之庭"或"学之园"。这可能是因为无论是庭还是园，都孕育着各自的故事，学校的环境受到来自周边的妥善守护，因而得此美名。学生们在各自所属的学校体验三到六年的校园生活，并在那里积存起各种回忆的点滴。学校对未来的自己来说，就是一座感怀过去的"记忆公园"。

　　以下介绍的日本和中国的三所大学，立地条件都较有优势。作为教育景观，除了设定必要的空间，还要配置能够留存在学生心中的丰富空间。有必要推行把在场地内发生的行为也融入设计的景观规划。

　　From old days in Japan, schools have been expressed as "garden of learning." Probably, it is because there is a common quality as places of nurturing in enclosed environment. Students will spend from 3 to 6 years at the college campus. Many memories will be accumulated there and will be a "garden of memories" to reminisce in the future.

　　The three universities in Japan and China in these pages are relatively blessed in locations. Needless to say, we have incorporated every necessary element for the landscape of education, but also proposed various designed spaces for the enrichment of campus life and its memories to be harbored for a lifetime.

中京大学农田校舍

尾道大学校园

大连医科大学校园

Chukyo University Toyota Campus

中京大学农田校舍

Toyota, Aichi, 2007

　　该设计以校园总体规划为基础，提出了两个充分利用地形的设计方案。首先是把位于大学本部的中心广场设计成"丘之景"，运用几何学的形态，构成极具象征性的空间。在广场中心按阶梯状挖一个圆形的水池，在左右两侧设置延伸至水池的长条形平台，为学生们提供在此站立、聚集等可供交流的空间。相对于周围那些有着明显时光痕迹的建筑，景观则通过铺装样式、网格化栽种的基调，井井有条地展开。此外，盈盈绿色的林荫小道作为连接广场的道路，是与雕刻家共同创作的一条小道。原运动场的空间作为"原野之景"，在此设置有机并具有环游性的散步和锻炼路线。园内道路利用水池、小溪、地形起伏变化和植栽，展现出多姿的景观。

　　旨在把广场建设成一个和水与绿相亲的场所，在这里光影交错，心神舒缓的宁静氛围油然而生。

Two landscape designs conforming to the landform was proposed based on a materplan of the campus. First of the two is the center plaza including campus headquarter planned as a "hill landscape" and applying geometric patterns into a highly symbolic designs. The half bridged stages on the perfect circle shaped pond at center of the plaza were devised as a lounging and communication space for the students. In contrast to the architectures of previous time, landscape design was developed in orderly grid pattern for the paving and plantings. The promenade into the plaza was designed in the image of a shady grove in collaboration with a sculptor. The other landscape where athletic field was is a "meadow landscape" designed in organic patterns with strolling and jogging courses. With a pond, a stream, and undulation of landform covered in greenery, rich diverse landscape is devised. The space aimed to offer commune with water and greenery has become a relaxing space where lights and shade cross.

Further proposal is being drafted today to incorporate the surrounding rural landscape into such plans as eco-terrace made available to the community as well.

对面页：广场中央圆形池，树木与周围建筑的意向极为得体地融合，创造出独具特色的风景。

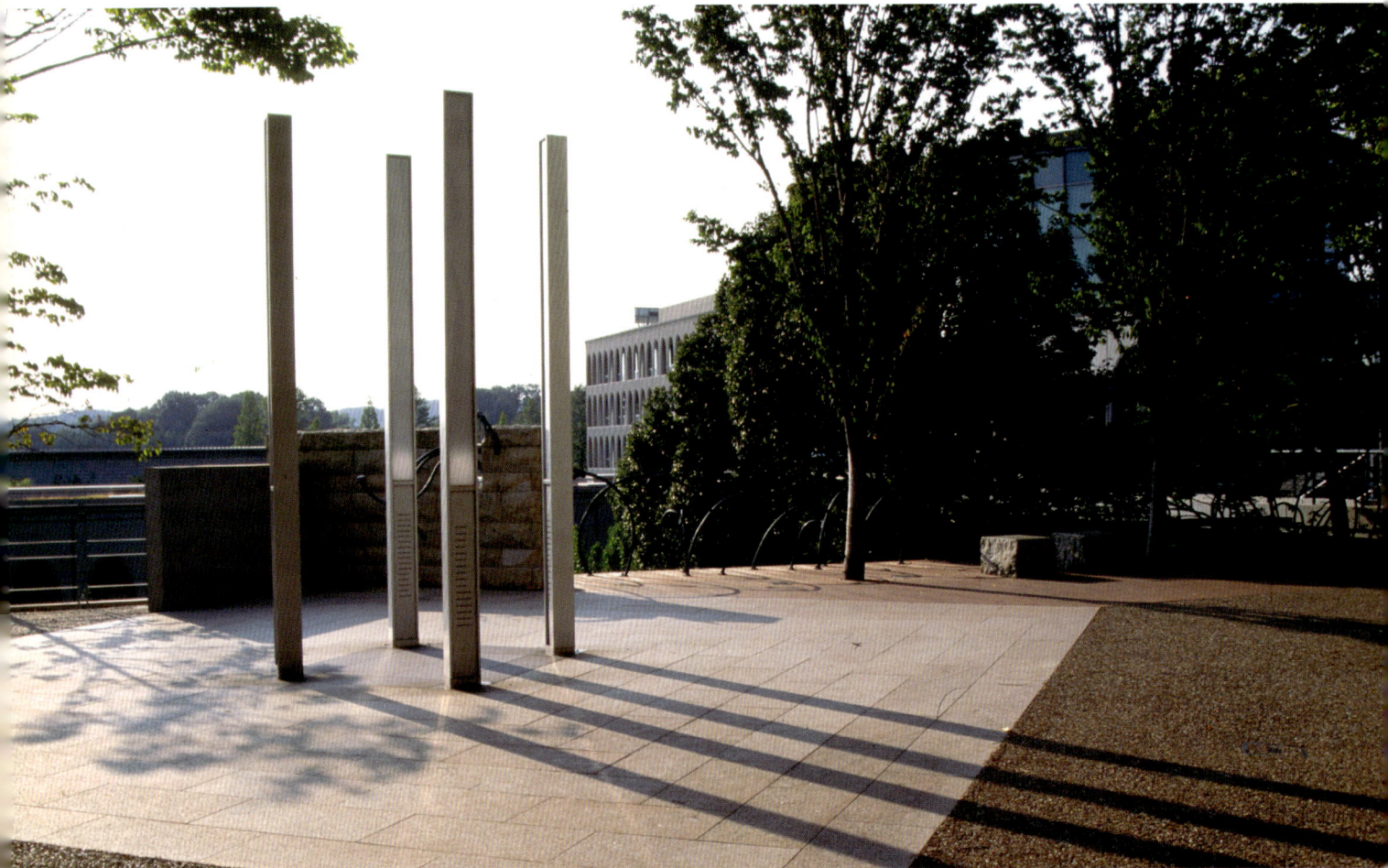

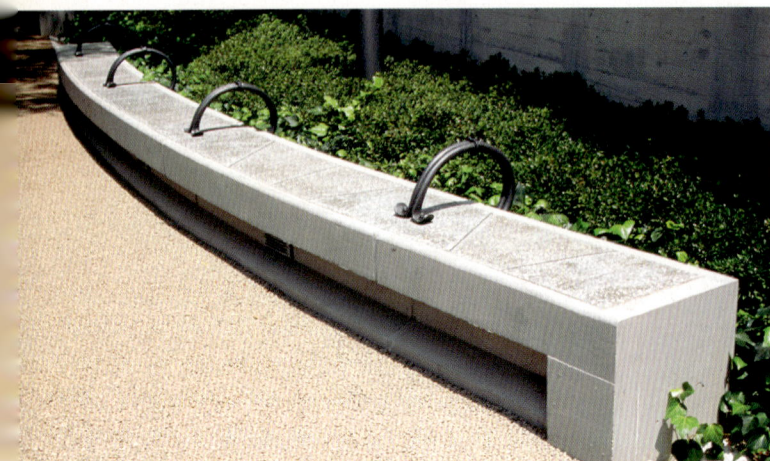

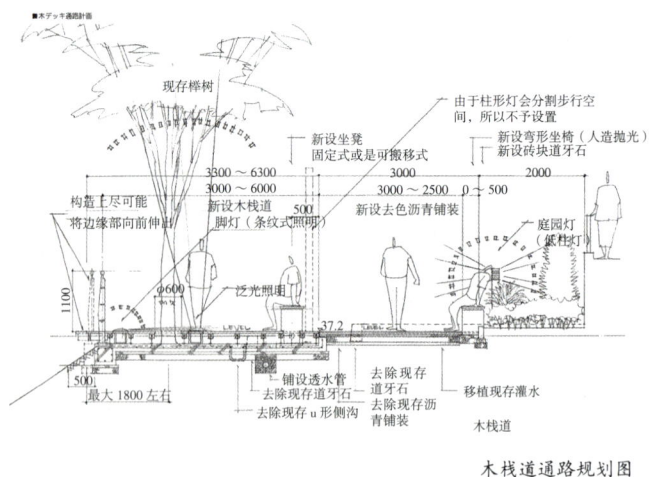

■木デッキ通路計画

现存榉树

由于柱形灯会分割步行空间，所以不予设置

新设坐凳 固定式或是可搬移式

新设弯形坐椅（人造抛光）
新设砖块道牙石

3300～6300
3000～6000

3000

3000～2500　0　500

2000

构筑上尽可能将边缘部向前伸出

新设木栈道
脚灯（条纹式照明）

500

新设去色沥青铺装

庭园灯（低柱灯）

1100

0600

泛光照明组

37.2

铺设透水管
去除现存道牙石

去除现存道牙石
去除现存沥青铺装

移植现存灌水

木栈道

500

最大1800左右

去除现存u形侧沟

木栈道通路规划图

用四盏雕塑般的照明灯构成"林荫小道"的终点。长凳、扶手是与铁艺造型艺术家小峰贵芳共同创作。

At the terminal of "Grove Promenade" are four pillars of outdoor lights creating sculptural image. The cast iron benches and handrails are products of collaboration with the iron craft artist, Takayoshi Komine.

连接散步小道宽
幅阶梯处的扶手
和四根照明柱的
形成较好的对比
效果好

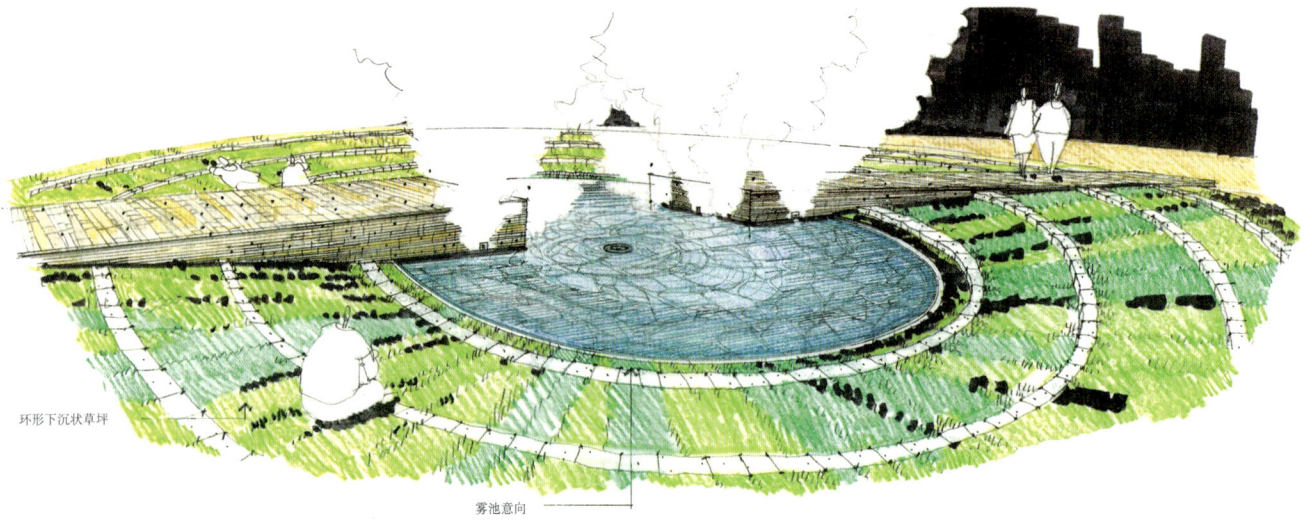

环形下沉状草坪

雾池意向

- 雾喷嘴：5个×2处
- 池水循环设备1套
- 过滤设备1套
- 水井设备（利用现有设备）
- 安装金属防护物

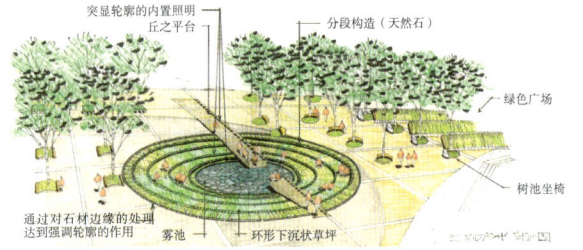

突显轮廓的内置照明
丘之平台

分段构造（天然石）

绿色广场

通过对石材边缘的处理
达到强调轮廓的作用

雾池

环形下沉状草坪

树池坐椅

小丘平台意向图

在圆形设计中放入直线的要素，为周围的格状铺装带来变化。

"丘之广场"位于圆形地块的中心，突出周边网格模式铺装的向心性。水池向中心处下沉，围聚在此的人们互相对望，创造交流的机会。伸向池心的平台演绎隆重大气的氛围，同时，相对于"原野广场"展现景观轴的特性。

The Hill Plaza is designed in simple grid pattern to provide formalness as an entrance to the campus headquarters. It was successful to have taken abstemious design method for the purpose of integrating diverse angles of the architectures.

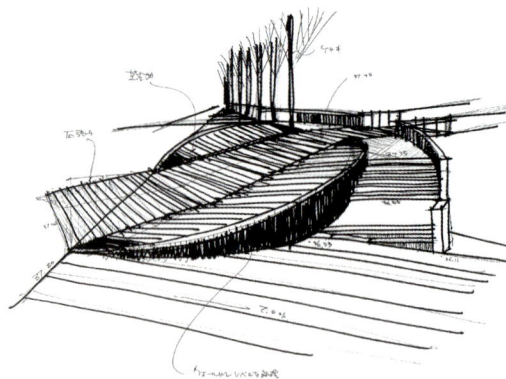

广场的纹理，从太阳开始斜射的时候开始，流溢美感和存在感。树荫和道路的反射光为广场多层次的景观添光加彩。

The texture of the plaza intensifies its existence in the late afternoon. The shade of the trees and reflecting sunlight on the paving support the impression of multi-layered landscape.

延伸至新校舍的广场与草坪的美景

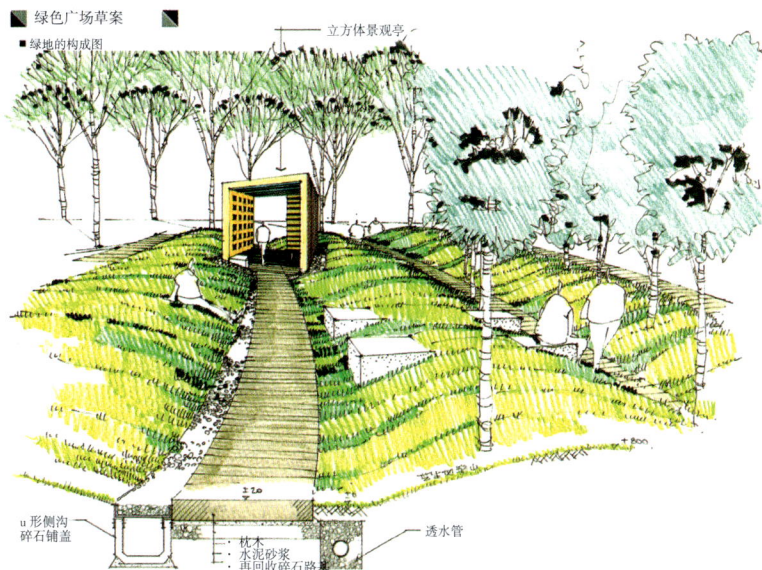

绿色广场"草坪隆起和立方体景观亭"

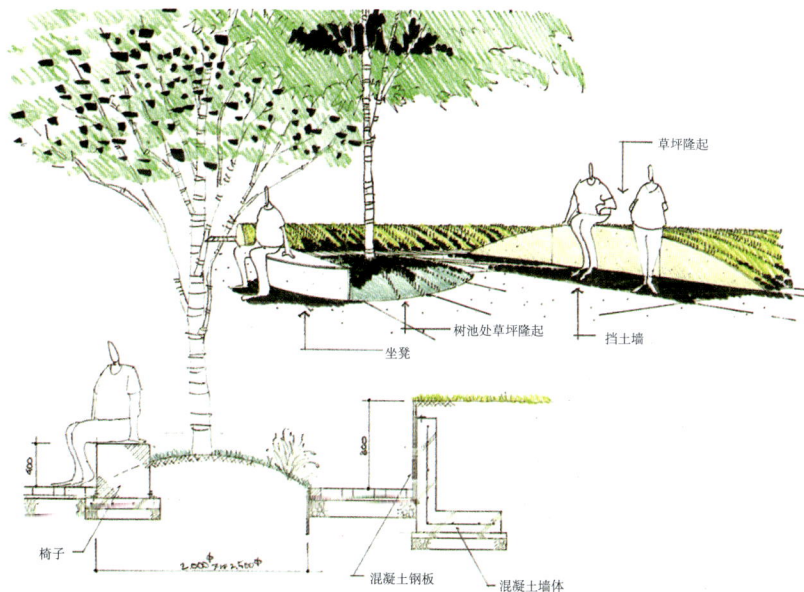

圆形树池、凳椅及树池处隆起的草坪

"细节尽显神韵"是设计的原则。在细小的地方进行缜密地布置，可以提升整体的美感。尤其在材料种类变化的地方，设计时必须格外注意。

It is a common sense for the designers that "god descends to details." Careful detailing adds perfection to the whole. Especially, where the different materials meet need special attention to the details.

下部草坪空间的平台，夕阳的光线为空间平添一份神秘与内涵。

用圆形和正方形的简单设计表现形状复杂的"丘之广场"。通过多层圆形从大到小的尺寸变化，表现场景的推移，而通过细致纹理修饰的网格则体现场景的秩序性。

The "Hill Plaza" having complex landform is described by simple circle and rectangle design patterns. Various sizes of circles from small to large represent transitions of the space, and the grid with delicate textures express orderliness.

"原野广场"突然一变，采用了连续的柔和曲线的设计，为平面形态带来了立体的丰腴感，深化了空间的质感和软化的效果。

Comparatively, continuous gentle curves are the design features of "Meadow field". The quality of the space has deepened by imposing a three-dimensional swelling into a two-dimensional form, and the effect of softness is emphasized.

建筑物附近的景观设计应该减小规模，用细腻的纹理与之对应。这里，相对于长凳形成的舒缓曲线，通过细致的木质铺装与其形成对比。

The landscape design close to the building should be reduced in the expression of scale and should correspond with detail texture. The contrast compliments the bench that draws a gradual curve by detailed wood paving.

桥是园内道路连续风景中不可或缺的场景。桥的周边要做到没有视野障碍，作为观望点，这一点十分重要。同时作为观望的焦点，有必要研究好观望点，对饰景做充分地考虑。

One of the essentials in the sequence of walking path is a bridge. As a view point there should not be any obstacles in the vicinity to block the view. At the same time, bridge is a point of focus of the landscape. Therefore, viewing point should be studied with care in relation to the scenery.

有效地利用规划前就有的现存树木十分重要，这也是设计者的一个乐趣所在。中京大学的历史和经历的时间，通过历经风雪的大树和薪新校舍的对比，似曾相识地表现出来。

Utilizing existing trees is important and is intriguing to the designers. The contrast between an aged tree and newly built architecture seems to represent the history of Chukyo University and passing of time.

总体规划平面图

时间和空间

学生时代可能会突然面对停课等比较空闲的时间。起劲儿地和朋友聊天，吹着舒心的风，无所事事地等着时间过去也是一种不错的选择。这个时候有一个出色的景观空间是何等的幸福。学生们期待在大学校园内发现一块自己喜欢的天地，并加以利用。为此，景观设计师必须营造一个经得起长时间逗留的高品质的多彩空间。在此基础上如果能配备可供选择的各种各样的空间，那么在学生时代度过的时光将成为一生的珍宝。

Time and Space

In student life, unexpected spare time arises with cancellation of classes or alike. Time could be consumed in conversations with friends, but just idling in relaxation, feeling the gentle breeze may be a precious time to spend. And how marvelous it is that there is a favorite pleasant spot in the campus landscape that is always there for you. Therefore, the landscape architects are obliged to contribute enduring space of timeless quality. With diverse choices of spots provided, the days of rich campus life would be a memory cherished for lifetime.

从入口广场至丘之广场的园路，通过材质的变换创造此处独有的空间。

Onomichi University Campus

尾道大学校园

Onomichi, Hiroshina, 2007

大学位于濑户内海边一个名叫"尾道"的小城市，远离市中心。对于这样一个地处尾道却感觉不到尾道风味的校园，不知学生们会有何感想。若能在校园中表现出尾道的历史与文化，学生们一定能够更加切身地感受到在尾道学习的氛围。

于是，为达到下述目的，对设计进行了挑战。隐喻地表现尾道蕴含的各种地方性事物，从而使景观设计不仅能够展现尾道的历史、文化与产业，同时让学生们在校园里感受到尾道风情。

- 尾道的自然

利用延伸至湖畔的草坪缓坡，抽象地表现出山与海的关联性。

- 尾道的海

利用延伸至湖中的木平台及船帆状的小品，表现出漂浮在海面上的帆船景象。

- 尾道的历史

将附近神社的鸟居（注：标志着神社入口处的门框）作为轴线的一部分，表现出古今事物的对比。

- 尾道的文化

在连续的壁面上分别涂上红白两色，象征了古建筑中的色彩对比（印度红的柱子和白色墙体）。

- 尾道的农作物

在配有坐凳的树池内种植柑橘类植物，象征了硕果累累的大学生活。

人与景相遇并融入其中，成为风景的一部分。创造出一个能够让学生们终身怀念在校园中度过的多彩时光的风景，这不就是作为一名景观设计师的职责吗？

A small city on the coast of Seto Inland Sea, Onomichi is an historic port well known for having staged many novels and films. The university campus is located far off the central part of city and had lacked any cultural references to the town of Onomichi. In thus, the design developed was laminating contexts unique to Onomichi as metaphor into the landscape where history, culture and industry could be felt.

Natural landscape of Onomichi: the mountains and sea represented by grass hill and pond

Sea of Onomichi: naval image expressed by the deck and monument

History of Onomichi:Torii gate of the neighboring shrine was incorporated into the view from the plaza

Culture of Onomichi: wall colors of cinnabar red and white reference colors of old temples

Industry of Onomichi: citrus orchard to symbolize fruitful school life

One meets a landscape, embraced by it, and one becomes the landscape. The blessed time on the campus will go by, and landscape that would be remembered and cherished for a long time by the students is the task to be fulfilled by the landscape architects

对面页：与池相邻的广场中设置了作为学生休憩空间用的凳椅、表现扬帆之舟的小品以及木制平台。这些将广场营造成一个标志性的空间。

在植栽地前端堆起土丘，
视作小山，向湖呈下斜
状，形成山与水的关联。
选用与水景相衬的月桂
树种植在轴线上，风中
摇摆的树姿形成一道美
丽的风景线。

Embankment was formed
in front of the planting
area to slope down
towards the lake to create
relation of mountain and
water. Rows of Katsura
trees (cercidiphyllum
japonicum) to represent
landscape of water were
planted along the axis.

顶部凹凸的铁板围成半圆形，形成一个广场，不仅为学生提供穿行的功能，而且与配套的格状凳椅一起，满足聚集与休息的功能。学生们随意地走走停停，时而闲聊的身姿传递着轻松悠闲的校园氛围。

Jagged rusted iron plates arranged in semicircle to suggest access circulation and with benches placed in grid, lounging area is furnished. Relaxed atmosphere of the campus can be observed by the students coming and going, stopping, and in conversations.

在连续的白墙中，将神社的鸟居（入口处标志性构筑物）作为见证
历史的象征物，引入景观。

连续的粉色墙体

横穿广场的斜墙，根据投来视线的角度，呈现"白色壁面"或"浅桃色壁面"。墙体由连接山与湖的斜挡土坡构成，白色象征寺院的白墙，浅桃色则象征寺院圆柱的红。过道作为休憩空间，配置了与墙体高度相协调的凳椅等设施。

The walls crossing the plaza are either "white wall" or "pink wall" depending on the side of the view. The walls are, functionally, retaining walls against the slope descending to waterfront. The white color symbolizes the white walls of temple, and the pink color represents cinnabar red paint of wooden columns of architecture. The aisles also serve as place of lounging. The locations of the benches are adjusted according to the height differences of the walls.

铁板的形态与其后的山峦重叠，中心的造型小品如同被包裹一般。

广场入口的步行空间，以规整种植的行道树、暗示后部广场纹样的铁板以及混凝土墙，构成一个整体。

The promenade space by the entrance area is structured by the composition of regularly planted trees with iron and concrete walls metaphorically suggesting the textures of the plaza in the rear.

尾道造船厂的"锈铁板"放置在广场的中央。铁板不仅标示了广场的领域，同时，上部精细的曲线模拟了周边群山的姿态。铁板被时间慢慢锈蚀着，散发出它独特的韵味。

"Rusted iron plates" seen at Onomichi shipyards are arranged in the center of the plaza. The plates signify the territory, and at the same time, the jagged edges represent the skyline. With passing of the time the corrosion will deepen, and the texture unique to this material will be further enhanced.

隐喻

隐喻是指采用非直接的手法表现事物。本项目中，将一个拥有悠久历史的海边小镇的风情，间接地在一个完全不相关的空间中展现出来。"故事性"在景观设计中极为重要。将土地自古以来传承的历史、文化、艺术、产业等用不同的形式在当今得以再现，即，把"隐喻"作为方法论进行使用的例子较为常见。"隐喻"设计手法，可能不会立即得到人们内心的共鸣；但是，通过经久反复地体会，一定能感悟到其中的寓意。

Metaphor

Metaphor is an indirect implication of an image. Here, an image of quaint historic city by the sea is indirectly expressed in a totally different location and space. Narrative is an essentiality in landscape design. Oftentimes, a method of metaphor is taken to revive in different forms the local history, culture, industry, etc. There is a possibility that the metaphor will not reach out and be recognized immediately. Nevertheless, by repeated experiences and passing of time, it will eventually be perceived.

Dalian Medical University Campus

大连医科大学校园
Dalian, China, 2008

作为 21 世纪学园都市的领军项目，大连医科大学的校园坐落于大海之滨、阳光普照的雄伟山丘之上。以"生命之景观"为理念，旨在营造出一个属于医科大学的学习环境。万名学子生活的校园，不只是单纯的大学用地，而且还是"街区"。因此，本案把具有统一感的街区作为目标，充分利用"天空"、"大海"和"山丘"的资源进行景观规划。

布局理念：将始于山止于海的南北向主轴作为主脊，而东西向配置的建筑群则由水平向的东西轴相连，让纵横轴相互交错。从门楼开始逐渐抬升坡度，以总部大楼为顶点，面向大海，设置纵向延伸的南北轴。这两条轴线是景观的骨架，多样化的设计在此展开。

形态理念：规划一个具有 110 公顷规模的景观，构架一个与之相称的布局的同时，还需要有一个保持空间统一感的设计基调。在此，以"生命之景观"为主题，采用了与生命体有关的灰岩坑（Doline）的形态。灰岩坑是在石灰岩地质区域中发现的直径达 20 米的圆形的下陷洼地。作为与周围相隔绝的空间，洼地存在着独立的生态系统，可以说是如"生命之卵"般的一个空间。我们在守护"生命"的大学校舍之间设计了各种形态的灰岩坑。

质感理念：建筑群富有国际化风情，而景观则充分利用当地素材构建延伸至海的轴线，达到创建富有风土气息的目标。将本地的大地色系的石材，以薄片堆积的形式，呈南北向摆放在作为主轴的草坪广场之上；东西轴则用当地出产的花岗石强调轴性设计。植物栽植，一部分树木是从老校区移植而来，同时挑选与气候相适宜的树种，力争使景观与周围环境相协调。

Identified as a leading project of academic city of the 21st century, Dalian Medical University campus site is a magnificent sunny hill overlooking the ocean. "Landscape of life" as a concept, we aimed to create an academic environment of a medical university. The campus where over 10,000 students reside is not just a campus grounds, but it is a "city" in a sense. Therefore, making of a unified city incorporating the resources of the "sky", the "sea", and the "hill" was objected.

Concept of framework As for structural framework of the site, the mountains toward sea (north-south) main axis is connected and related to the architectures arranged horizontally on the east-west axis. From the gate towards the headquarter building, in gradual ascending slope, the vertical north-south axis opens out to the sea. Within the two axis structuring the landscape, diverse designs were developed.

Concept of forms In a large-scale project of 110ha as this, it is essential to have an accurate structural framework and at the same time, unified design foundation is vital. In conforming to the theme of "landscape of life," doline with organic relevance was addressed. Doline is a natural depression or hole in the surface topography of limestone region caused by the removal of soil or bedrock, often both, by water. These depressions disconnected from the surrounding environment have peculiar ecological system, so to speak, "eggs of life" like space. Various designs of doline were applied in the spaces between the buildings of university where protection of "life" is the agenda.

Concept of texture Although the architectures are of international style, landscape design aimed to highlight the local climate utilizing local resources. Earthen colored header bond wall of local stones stretches on the north-south axis along the grass lawn, and east-west is emphasized by the granite paving. Plants were partially transplanted from the old campus, with selection of trees suiting the climate, landscape in congruous to the surrounding environment was contrived.

对面页：从总部大楼处看到的正门、其后的街区及山岳，与入口大楼复杂的构造相对应，采用了简洁、平面的景观设计。

大学的正门采用具有透明感的卵形设计，按照从门框处向总部大楼仰望般的感觉来建造。因为有众多的人使用总部大楼的前庭，所以将空间平坦化，并以条形设计和10根景观柱塑造一个象征性的空间。

From the gate frame of the main entrance with transparent oval structure, headquarter over the slope can be observed. The front courtyard of the headquarter building is symbolically designed having flat space in simple stripe patterned pavement with structures of 10 pillars.

从总部楼广场处遥望正门

总体规划平面图

正面山丘上左右成列栽种着针叶树，代表着大学的有序治学，其背后则配置了较为柔和的植栽。相对于建筑中随意设计的柱子，采用重复设置的水平状铁板与之相对应，形成对比。

On the slopes of either side are planted with rows of evergreen trees to express academic orderliness, and softer vegetation in the rear. Repetition of horizontal steal boards is in contrast to the random design of the architectural columns.

从广场处看到的总部大楼架空层

从总部大楼平台眺望广场与大海，过于弱小的树木无法达到设计效果。

透过广场眺望总部大楼平台。

东西向的长条和有一定角度的南北轴线，勾勒出总部大楼南部的广场。中央处的图案顶部呈开阔状，描绘了一幅整个大学校园面向大海、开阔的景观。

The plaza square on the south of the headquarter building is expressed with the stripes running east to south angled by the north-south axis. The pattern design in the center spreading out at the end is in the image of campus site landscape opening out to the sea.

东西两侧建筑之间形成的中央空间，面向大海，场景恢宏。功能性的动线设置在建筑物一侧，通过树木、流水、铺装、堆石，让广场的表情得以尽现。

The central space between the buildings of east and west has a wide landscape opening out to the sea. With most of the functional circulations included into the architectural space, diverse expressions of the plaza are composed by the trees, water channel, paving, and stone structures.

从总部大楼眺望南部校园，大气壮美的风景映入眼帘。

这个山丘是学生宿舍区。大门为大学创立时所建，从旧址迁移而来。希望以此传承珍惜历史物件、有效加以再利用的精神。

This hill is an area for student residences. The gate brought from the old site was built when the university was first established. It is hoped the spirit to value historic objects will be succeeded.

从教学区的阶梯处眺望雕塑小品及商业设施地形的变化因建筑物的存在而更现直观。

山丘上是老师和同学们休憩的场所。在景色优美的坡顶设置休息场所，可以让人们在此享受安逸的时光。
Atop the hill is a relaxing area for the teachers and students. A resting space with a view was prepared for their break times.

因其位置依山面海，所以在这个节点上更加凸显了对海的设计。通过对海平面及立体剪裁，人们与更显俊逸的海在此相遇。
As the site location is on a slope facing the sea, the design to emphasize ocean was taken. By framing the sea horizontally, sharpness of the sea is highlighted.

采集、选用当地的天然石材作堆积景观墙。尽管堆积地域材料的方式极为质朴，但重要的是将这样的理念展现给人们。
This is a header bond wall of stones collected locally. It is a simple structure of piled natural stones, but there is significance in being shown as so.

重视雨水的自然形态，尽量不使用土木设施。
The flow of water respects the importance of its naturalistic form, mitigating excess engineering maintenance.

医科大学以救死扶伤为宗旨，所以采用椭圆的形态和柔和的立体物件来表现"生命"。

As the university deals with matters of life, many references were made to "life" in oval patterns and organic formed objects.

在建筑中间留意设计人性化尺度的景观。用低矮的护墙对高低差进行处理，和植物共同形成富有设计性的景观。

For spaces between the buildings, careful consideration was made to design the landscape in human scale. Level changes are treated by low height walls, and along with plantings, a landscape of design proficiency was sought.

在南部营造了生态空间，从那里仰望时看到的校园如同一幅大尺度的立体宽银幕全景画面。

Biotope area has been fixed at the south area. The campus viewed from here is a grand panorama.

封闭的空间，开放的空间

大连医科大学的校园是一个开放的空间。这里不仅有开放式的运动设施和开敞的场地，还拥有广袤的海岸线。这样的郊区校园，缺少与市民和当地人们交流的场所。本次景观设计有效地利用了地形特征，设置了七座山丘、水池、生态环境、流水等。随着时间的推移、树木的生长，校园将变得越来越美丽，期望各种各样交流在此诞生。

Closed space, Open space

The campus of Dalian Medical University is an opened space. It has to opened sports facilities, open space, and coast. Such suburbs type is few and communication spaces of the citizens and people in the region are few on campus. In this landscape, the shape of land is effectively used, and seven hill, pond, biotope, and the flows, etc. are arranged. It is hoped the tree grows up as years pass, and various communications are generated in the campus that became more beautiful.

从规划用地的最南部仰望校园，在缓缓倾斜的南坡强调水平线的同时，让建筑和景观融合，描绘出充裕的风景。

In Japan, many efforts are now being made in preserving and restoring old traditional houses as being done in China. As well as architectures, gardens and surrounding landscape are being reproduced incorporating its original style and form. One example is a traditional house relocated into a large-scale park and recovered as a newly arranged park facility. The other is a restoration project of existing old house and reviving the ruined landscape. Either project would not have been successful without the understandings from.

The garden project at Schönbrunn Palace in Vienna expresses a dream of the Japanese people. Mutual sense of respect and appreciation for history in the both countries has made this restoration project possible.

一之江名人山宅

本乡富士山公园

森柏龙宫殿的日本庭园

Ichinoe Nanushi Yashiki

一之江名人古宅
Edogawa, Tokyo, 1999

　　景观设计不仅仅是创新，对历史上留存下来的古迹进行修复、创造出能够迎合现代需求的项目也是景观设计的重要工作。久经风雪时迁，坐落于东京都江户川区一之江的田岛家古宅现已成为当地的标志性建筑。（田岛家曾任当地的新田政策指导人，现存的主屋于安永三年重建，即公元1774年）。1992年曾对古宅进行解体重修，1999年完成古宅的景观设计，南庭、入口庭园、古宅林地、耕地遗址以及沟渠等修复工程。

　　本规划不仅对古宅进行了复原与修建，还将古宅建设成一个能够满足一般游客多种需求的场所。以"名主古宅生活风情"为主题，融汇了以下内容。

　　•庭园方面　以南庭为题材介绍庭园

　　对庭园与主屋连为一体的历史遗迹进行了复原。让游客们体验昔日名主的生活风貌，同时将其作为学习日本庭园鉴赏方法以及庭园史的教材。

　　•园艺方面　以庭园及古宅林地的花草为题材

　　在庭园内栽种了自江户时代起就生长在这一地区的植物，并种植了昔日流行的园艺植物，使来访的游客们能够体验到"名主古宅岁月记"。

　　•生态方面　介绍古宅林地及庭园生物的环境共生

　　复原周边环境，为生物提供可以繁殖的栖息地，作为环境教育的场所。

For landscape architects, to restore and establish new programs matching the needs of today for the inherited landscape is an important calling as designing a new landscape. Tajima family estate built in 1774, once was a residence of the leading figure of farming land development, has survived the centuries and exists as a local symbol in Edogawa of Tokyo. The house was dismantled and repaired in 1992, and restoration of the landscape with the gardens, forest, farmland and moats were completed at 1999.

Rather than simply restoring the site, it was made into a project with a theme of "landscape of life at the Nanushi Yashiki (estate of the village head)" with diverse programs open to the public. The contents are as follows:

• Garden program: introduction of south garden

Restore integrated garden and the main quarter of historic interest to provide visitors to experience the

• life style of the past and Japanese garden education

Gardening program: introduction of plants in the garden and the forest

• Plant native species common to the Edo period as well as the garden trend of the era, and experience seasonal cycles at the Nanushi Yashiki

• Ecology program: introduction of wildlife found in the garden and the forest, ecological symbiosis

Restore natural environment to provide and induce wildlife habitation for ecology education

对面页：

作为庭园主要景观的瀑布位于南部面北的位置。虽然当初的立石已倒，落水石的位置也难以确定，还是将其仔细地发掘出来并进行复原。尽管根府川石鲜少被用作组石的石材，但因其棱角鲜明的造型，决定在本项目中使用。结果证明，根府川石成功地展现了竖向的设计，勾画出令人满意的多样姿态。

The waterfall, which is the main focal element of the garden, is located in the south part of the garden facing north. At the beginning, the tateishi, vertical stone which is a side stone symbolizing the steepness had fallen, and the mizuochi-ishi, the key stone symbolizing the cascade had been lost, but after thorough excavation, the waterfall was revived. The stones were Nebuka-ishi, type of andesite normally not used for stone arrangements, but for the sharp rugged features, we elected to use. The verticality was emphasized and a satisfactory distinctive design was achieved as the result.

对于传统风味的古宅大门，景观设计需显厚重。斜向延伸至大门的道路铺设了大块花岗岩，在仿如框中画似的中庭里种植了松树。相对于建筑，周围的树木繁茂得恰到好处，很好地展现了具有悠久历史的景观。

Stately landscape design is indispensable to compliment the traditional gate. The access path is structured with large granite, and pine trees in the picture frame of the inner courtyard. Thickness of the trees agrees with the subdued atmosphere of historic architecture.

在从主屋回望大门方向的构图中，将主要树木种植在门户空间中央，形成标志。设计时让宽广的园路以及石材的重量感来承受屋顶设计的厚重感。

In the composition of mikaeri method towards the gate from the main quarter, a key tree is planted at the center of the gate making it the landmark. Against the hefty image of the roof, receptive design was contrived by ample width of the path and massiveness of the stones.

目前中庭在过去曾被作为农耕地使用，未曾种植树木等任何景观植物。此次规划中，种植了松树以及梅树，以示吉祥。无论怎样在中庭取景，建筑与作为背景的高大树林都搭配得完美无缺。惹人注目的中庭人工植栽是此园的特色。

As the courtyards were traditionally a space for farming chores, there were neither trees nor objects of ornamental purposes existed. However for this courtyard, to express auspices, pine and plum trees were planted. Viewing from any direction, the tall trees in the rear and the architectures are in perfect proportion characteristically complimenting the contrived space of the courtyard.

从庭园处看建筑的主屋。

主屋东部设有小规模的地泉环游式庭园。为保留原有地基、修复时将主屋抬高了50厘米，整个庭院也相应地填土抬高。虽然庭园的修建年份不详，但从在江户时代的古庭园风格——池泉旁沙洲放置汀步以及雪见灯笼的设计来看，这里的庭院景观虽是小景，却亦堪称佳作。院中多丛枝生的米槠树在古宅建设之初就已经存在。据传，家主从武士成为地主的时候，将自己的武器埋在这棵树下。

There existed a small stroll garden on the east of the main quarter. In order to maintain the old foundation of the main quarter, the floor level was raised 50cm upon rebuilding. Consequently, the entire garden ground had to be raised by earth banking. It is not clear of how long the garden dates back, but it is created in a classic style of the gardens of Edo period with stepping stones along the water edge and yukimi style stone lantern. Although small in size, it is a finely made garden. There is a multi-trunked beech (castanopsis) tree existing since the beginning, and a legend is told that the master who became a townsman from samurai had buried his armors below the tree.

主屋庭园的石工艺品，石灯笼与三重石塔。

从室内可看到庭园中的设施，表现了庭园与建筑一体化的规划意图。尤其是反射在地板上的阳光，突显了地板的质感，使人产生一种期许在这里度过温馨时光的感觉。

The garden view from the rooms signifies the intended integration of the garden and architecture. The sunlight reflecting on the floor emphasizes its wooden texture creating a tempting atmosphere.

一之江名主古宅在庭院外还拥有宽广的杂木林，夏天时杂木林不仅阻挡了炎热的风，同时还吸引了小鸟昆虫等各种生物。从前这里的树枝曾被用作生火的薪材，落叶则作堆肥提供重要养分。

Besides the garden, Ichinoe Nanushi Yashiki has a span of forest where hot summer winds are blocked, and at the same time, having potential of attracting wild life as birds and insects. Moreover, in the old days, the forest was the source of firewood for fuel, and the fallen leaves were utilized as compost.

在古宅还有人居住的时候，这里的草坪曾被作为田地使用。想必当年主人餐桌上的多种蔬果食材，都从这里摘取。如今为省去管理上的麻烦，虽然这里不再用作耕地，但可考虑将此处作为地域活动的一个环节，让孩子们来此体验种植农作物。

The lawn area must have been a vegetable garden, and without doubt, its various fresh produce was delivered daily to the dining table of the household. The farm is not reinstated at this moment due to maintenance reasons, but it may be an idea to have the children experience farming as part of the local .

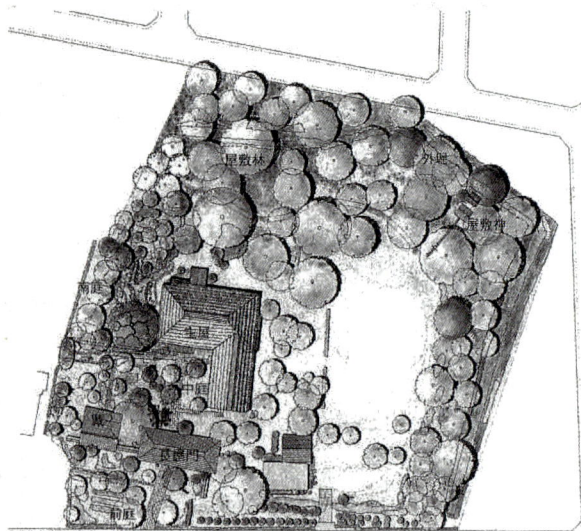

规划平面图

保护与利用

有效利用民居古宅的例子在逐渐增多。日本对寺院以及神社等文化遗产的保护已经趋向完整，现已逐步将民间的重要古宅列入保护对象。古宅的保护需要付出高昂的费用，如果缺少对其进行有效利用的方法，规划将落为空谈。可以将古宅作为举办只有旧式豪宅中才能进行的特别活动，或是将其作为展现传统文化的空间等加以利用。

preservation and utilization

Utilization of old traditional houses is often seen today. With law enforcement in preservation of cultural heritage as temples and shrines, private properties of historic values have become the subject of preserving as well. Nonetheless, preservations calls for great costs, it is essential to have specific plans of the reuse. There are many possibilities of functions and events, benefited by the oldness and fineness, as well as space to express our cultural heritage.

Hongo Fujiyama Park

本乡富士山公园

Yokohama, Kanagawa, 2003

本公园以形似富士山、标高为50米的"富士小山"为中心进行规划。周边区域虽已被开发成住宅用地，但该地区珍贵的植物绿地被完整地保留下来，对绿地加以利用，创造出符合市民的愿望、让游人留下深刻记忆、并值得骄傲的公园。

以"复原的民居古宅中体验乡土风情"为主题，根据用地的潜在价值将公园设置成两个区域。

1. 北区：有效利用移建、复原后的民居古宅，创造出能够让人体味里山（注：住家周围的山）生活以及本乡原有风貌的场所。

2. 树林区：充分利用保留完整的约5公顷丘陵地，在保护并继承绿化的同时，创造出人与自然以及生物近距离接触的场所。

作为与横滨市的合作项目，经过横滨市和荣区政府、市民及设计者之间的多次协商、会晤等合作，共同整理归纳出此次的建设规划。精心陈设了民居古宅周围的内院、外庭以及菜园等景观，以及面向背后的林地延伸自然的连续景观。移建过来的民居古宅建筑与周围的地形、树林环境相融合，形成了一种让人怀旧的里山景观。公园竣工后，市民们仍继续参与规划建设的各种活动、协同维护林中的制炭小屋、农田以及竹林。此外，草坪斜面的杂树林成为孩子们的游乐场所。

This park was planned focusing the "Fujiyama" mountain of about 50 meters in height resembling the shape of Mt. Fuji. The area was developed as residential district, nevertheless, in preservation and utilization of significant greenery, and in complying the wish of the community, aimed for a memorable park that the community would be proud of.

With the theme of "experiencing rural life at an old house," ascertaining the site potentiality, the park was composed into two areas:

1. North Area: relocate and restore an existing old residential house, and recreate a native rural scenery and life of Hongo.

2. Forest Area: preserve and utilize the hilly land (approx. 5ha) for sustaining greenery and wildlife.

As a partnership enterprise with the city of Yokohama, the project was carried out in cooperating body of city councils, resident community, and landscape architects. Around the old house was landscaped with an inner garden, outer garden, and a vegetable garden in sequence to the woods in the rear. The relocated house and other architectures are blended into the geography and surrounding forests, a quaint rural landscape was realized. The community participation is continued after the completion of the park in the maintenance of charcoal kiln, gardens, and bamboo forest. Moreover, the woods on the hillside are a great playground for the children.

对面页：集合了日本古代民宅美丽的屋顶，与屋后树林维拥的情景相融合的茅草屋顶是典型的日式风景。

面对民宅的日本庭园

民宅前的广场

庭园入口处

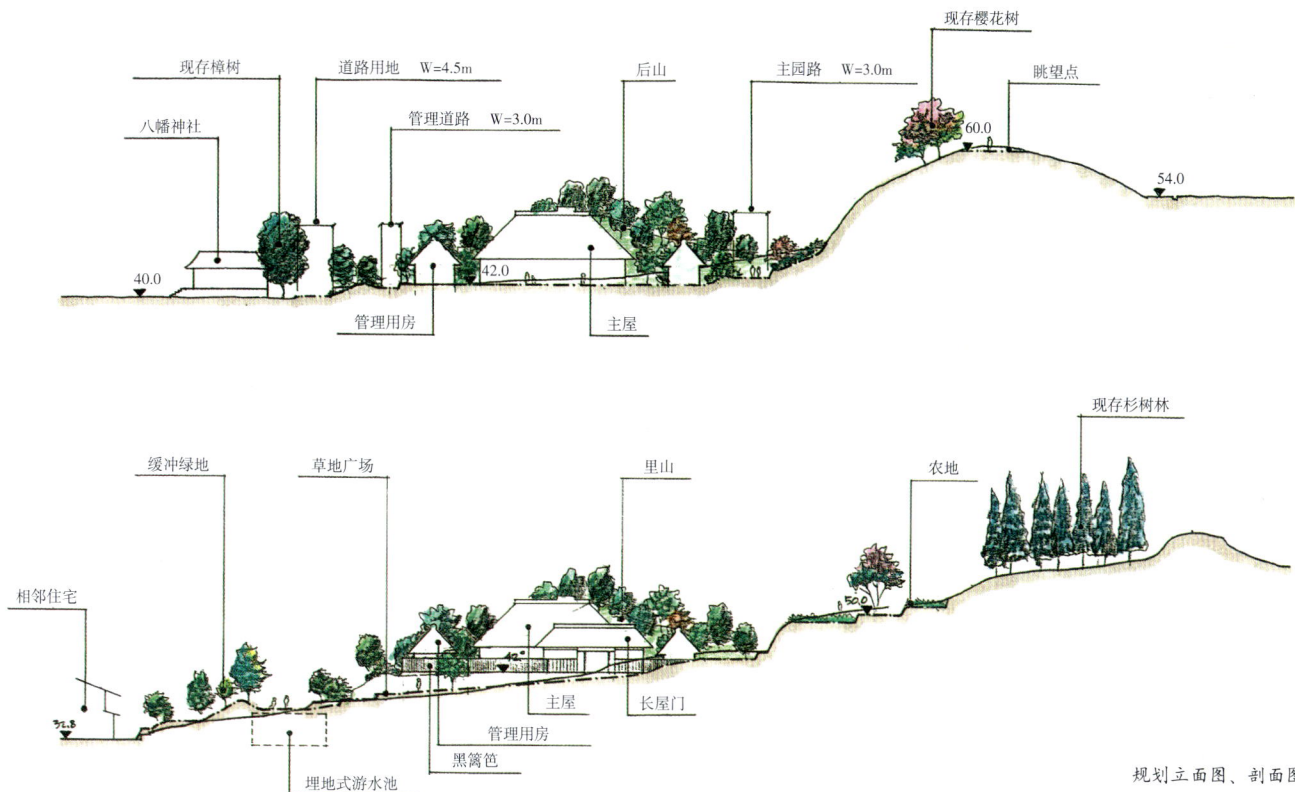

现存樟树　道路用地　W=4.5m　后山　主园路　W=3.0m　现存樱花树

八幡神社　管理道路　W=3.0m　眺望点

40.0　60.0　54.0

42.0

管理用房　主屋

现存杉树林

缓冲绿地　草地广场　里山　农地

相邻住宅

主屋　长屋门

埋地式游水池　黑篱笆　管理用房

规划立面图、剖面图

在此次规划中，成功地将古宅移建至半山腰的绝佳位置。以沉稳的屋顶以及水平线条作为设计基调是日本民居古宅的特征。长屋门式的古宅造型柔和，以美丽的姿态招呼着过往的路人。前庭则是用于农作等活动的场所。

The old house was relocated in the ideal location of a hillside. The distinctive features of old houses in Japan are the stately roofs and the emphasis of horizontal lines. The old house appearing through the frame of the gate is pleasing to the eyes and in perfect proportion entices us in. The front yard of the building is a space allotted for farming and various activities.

从长屋门眺望主屋

长屋门及其后的树林

总体规划平面图

在古宅的上方为志愿者们准备了活动的场所。栽培蔬菜的田地以及照片内侧可见的"制炭小屋"成为游园者重点光顾的场所。这些也是规划之初在研讨会上论证的活动项目，设计实施后形成的空间。

Above the old house are locations for various activities for the community volunteers. Farming allotment and the hut of charcoal kiln in the rear are the important venue for the people. This is a fine case study example of the realization of the proposed ideas from the start of the workshop.

农田夏日风景

农田冬日风景

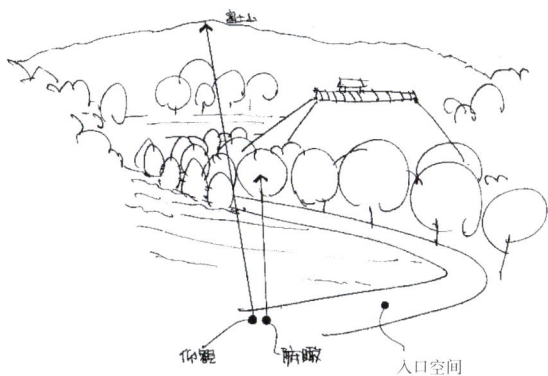

景观手绘图

公园里的园路由斜面配合连续的曲线形成。园路的构造使人们无法从大门入口处直接看到里面的建筑，只有沿着园路一路而下，拐过一个弯道时大屋顶才会突然出现在眼前。整个景观为人们带来一种惊喜。

The promenade of the park with controlled slope is composed in continuous gradual curves. The old house is hidden from the main entrances, and as walking along the descending path, a large roof of the house suddenly appears at a turn. It is an awe striking landscape.

环绕园内的蜿蜒园路

落叶风满情——园路秋景。

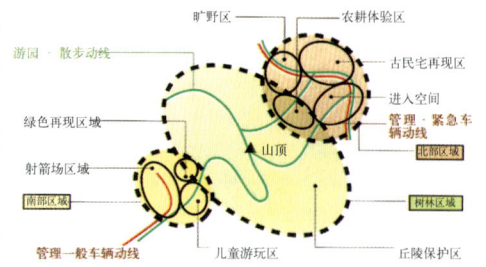

总体规划系统图

从山冈俯视古宅时可以看到两个大屋顶重叠在一起，与背后的树林相融，形成一幅典型的日式风景。

From the hilltop looking down, two large overlapping roofs integrated in the volume of the greenery of the natural forest is a typical Japanese landscape.

这里是连接住宅与田地的进入空间。沿原有自然林的林间空地拾级而上的阶梯以及右手边深处可见的"制炭小屋"，展现了一幅自然与人的和谐生活景象。

This shows the approaching path to the farming allotment from the old house. The climbing steps through the existing trees with the charcoal hut seen in the rear right is almost a description of life in the woods.

利用和参与

那些随着时代的变迁而不再经常使用的东西都曾面临被丢弃的命运。然而在近数十年里，或许是因为日本的发展告一段落，社会也趋向稳定的缘故，人们逐渐开始从历史事物中发掘价值。此次规划正是从"如何有效利用废弃的古民宅"的思考引发而来。如果没有当地居民的热情与努力，建造出来的可能只会是个普通的公园。为了思考如何利用古民宅，市民们发起研讨会，汇集了许多好主意。正是由于这个公园集思广益，因此开放后得到了民众的爱戴。

Utilization and Participation

Until quite recently, out-of-date or un-needed products were scrapped and thrown away. However, in these ten several years, it may be due to Japanese society having reached its maturity and settled, people have become to value things historical. The start of this project was deliberating how we could utilize the old house no longer functioned. If there were no enthusiasm and effort of the citizens, this park would have been just an ordinary park. For to utilize the ruined house, they initiated the workshop, and various ideas were proposed and compiled. This park is a product of the sprit of people in realizing what they "wish to do." Ever since the opening, the park is being appreciated by many.

Japanese Garden at Schönbrunn

森柏龙宫殿的日本庭园
Wien, Austria, 1998

　　奥地利首都维也纳的森柏龙宫殿里，拥有一座足可匹敌凡尔赛宫的雄伟、宽广的庭园。1997 年春天，在宽敞的巴洛克式庭园的一角，日本人偶然发现了一座看似被荒废的日本庭园。调查结果表明，这是 1913 年宫廷造园师们参考英国的日本庭园建造的。然而，随着 1914 年第一次世界大战的爆发，1918 年哈布斯堡家族统治结束，这座庭园就被长期地废弃，失去了往日风采。

　　1998 年，日本志愿者对这个庭园进行了修复。除去覆盖在庭园的植物和砂土，设组石、修池岸、调整泷石组、引水入池，庭园的修复工作顺利完成。此处的泷石组打破了日本传统格式呈直线性布局，成为连接与之紧邻的温室长轴的标志，将两部分设施很好地衔接在一起。

　　接到宫殿方面制作新的日本庭园的要求，在修复后的庭园的左边设置了枯山水，右边建造茶庭。枯山水采用了象征着日本和奥地利友好关系的鹤龟组石，以示吉祥；又因维也纳是音乐之都，所以设置了可以称为声音景观的水琴窟，路过的游客都惊叹不已。这里还蕴藏着其他的玄机，在砂面上勾绘出如同五线谱似的五条砂线，组石作为国歌的音谱配置其中。虽然这里用的石料、砂土、地衣都是从宫殿内和维也纳郊外采集而来，但作为日本庭园的材料却没有任何不和谐之感。

　　茶庭用仿龙安寺和建仁寺的篱笆围起，设置休息处、中门、洗手间、室外茶室、延段、汀步，采用正统的茶庭格局。为了让灯笼体现东西文化交流，选用了被称为耶稣灯笼的织部（注：一种陶制品）。这里的净手用水钵采用的是梵文中表现佛、被称为"四方佛"的石制品。设置在茶庭的入口处的"鹿吓"，其简洁的构造和自然的音色深受人们欢迎。

What seemed like a trace of Japanese garden was found unexpectedly in the baroque garden of Schönbrunn Palace in 1997. Through a research, it was identified that, in 1913, the superintendent of the palace gardens had created the garden referencing the one existing in England. However, in the following year the World War I had broke out, and this garden had been neglected for many years.

The restoration was carried out first by removing the plants and earth that had covered the entire garden, the stone arrangements and riparian works repaired, and waterfall composition was adjusted to run water for completion.

Further, a new kare sansui (dry landscape) garden with crane and turtle stone arrangement was created to the left of the original garden to commemorate Austria-Japan friendship. In associating Vienna as music capital, and suikinkutsu (water harp chamber) that may be called as an element of soundscape was installed, and drawing unexpected surprise of passers by.

On the right side of the garden, a teahouse is enclosed within Ryoanji and Kenninji style, bamboo fences. With a waiting, mid-gate, tsukubai washbasin, and steppingstones to outdoor teahouse, it is arranged in a complete formal style.

对面页：枯山水庭院及后方的大温室。

1920 年左右反映当时情景的珍贵照片。
Invaluable photograph portraying the image from the 1920s.

1998 年庭园修复完工。
Restoration was completed in 1998.

修复后重现昔日风姿的日本庭园。
正面，笔直的瀑布落入池水。在蜿蜒的汀步的右侧设有净手用水钵，近侧是仿金阁寺的竹篱。

Japanese garden restored to its original appearance.
The waterfall cascades straight into the pond at the center. On the right hand side of the steppingstones in drawing a curve, is a washbasin and seen in the foreground is Kinkaku-ji style bamboo fence.

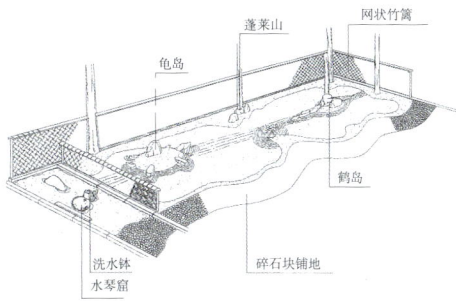

枯山水处手绘图

从维也纳近郊采集而来的石头，形态力度感强，富于变化，展现出日本庭园组石的豪快氛围。

The stones collected in the vicinity of Vienna are powerful in forms and varied in texture enabled an authentic Japanese stone arrangement, and a dynamic atmosphere was achieved.

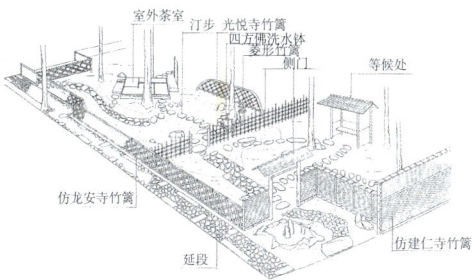

茶庭处手绘图

茶庭外部按举办正式茶道仪式的规范进行实施。用瓦铺设而成的四张半榻榻米大的空间里设置了床间（注：装饰用空间）和水屋（注：准备处），周围以竹篱围起，形成一个茶的世界。

The tea garden was arranged in specification fit for formal outdoor tea ceremonies. A four and a half tatami mat (approx. 4.5m²) space was paved with tiles, and with a tokonoma (alcove for ornaments) and a mizuya (preparation area), enclosed by bamboo fence a realm of tea is contrived.

规划平面图

屏风树立在床间（注：装饰用空间），摆放的装饰小品迎接着来宾。灯笼和净手用水钵是日本现代最顶级的石雕艺术家西村金造之作。

The ornamental objects placed before the screen at the tokonoma welcomes the visitors. The stone lantern and the washbasin were created by Kinzo Nishimura who is one of the top stone masons in Japan today.

用当地的石头铺设的园路、竹篱（龙安寺篱）

龟石组（前部）

茶庭入口处的门与鲤鱼旗

洗手钵与竹篱（沼津篱）

位于庭园一角的"鹿吓"，以其有节奏的动作和幽默的声音，愉悦着游客。另外还设置了"水琴窟"，一种埋入地中、欣赏落水声音的壶。

Rhythmical motion and humorous sounds of "Shishiodoshi (deer scarer)" delight the visitors. Moreover, a Suikinkutsu, a device to enjoy the echoing sound of water drip into a pot placed underground, has been installed here.

日本庭院传统的堆石、后侧是沼津垣。

好奇心

这是一个由数名充满"好奇心"的人聚集在一起完成的项目。首先是发现森柏龙宫殿内有不可思议空间的人。正是因为这份"好奇心"，他琢磨着"这个空间不会是一个日本庭园吧"，并且不远万里把这一消息传播到东京。而后又是因为"好奇心"，在没有任何确凿的参考资料的情况下，专家们专程造访奥地利。紧接着，当情况开始明朗，把它作为专题报道的 NHK 制片人也可以归属到有"好奇心"的一类。那是一篇卓越且内容极具创作性的报道。

虽说是一连串的偶然交叠才促成了这世纪性的发现，正是因为怀有"说不定很有趣"的好奇心，并马上付诸行动，才能获得如此成果。每每想起这个项目，我就在心中暗暗发誓：作为"物质空间"创造者的我们，永远都不能丧失这种"好奇心"。

Curiosity

This project was materialized by collective "curiosities" of people. Firstly was the person who found a mysterious space in the Schönbrunn Palace. The "curiosity" suspecting it might be a small garden was dispatched to far away Tokyo. And the professional researchers who flew in from Japan out of "curiosity" having only yet uncertain information are birds of a feather. Moreover, it must have been "curiosity" that drove the producers of NHK Broadcasting to film a documentary for their show. Incidentally, the show was of excellent quality.

A discovery of the century was made by several coincidental happenings. It is the mind to grasp "interest" which motivated to "react" brought the success of this project. As producers of "object spaces", whenever I think back over the project, I vow to myself never to lose this "curiosity".

Public parks accompanied with water feature create attractive and fascinating sceneries. From some reason, people tend to approach and touch water involuntarily. Is it because of water being the primary source of life – a foundation of daily life?

I believe that happiness of landscape design comes when the unconscious actions of site users were lured by the conscious intentions we designers take through design modification. To start of this dynamic project that involves detailed preparation of a 15km riverside alley, the first step was to design this Taibo Park. I would like to continue spending more time, for a high-quality design preparation.

无锡伯渎港河道环境景观

通过连接两个广场的门户桥梁营造城市面貌

泰伯文化广场意向图

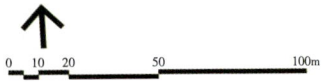

泰伯文化公园规划平面图（深化方案）

通常水位：3.06
平均最高水位：3.90
平均最低水位：2.69

通过连接两个广场的门户桥梁营造城市面貌

Riverside of Baidugang Wuxi

无锡伯渎港河道环境景观
Wuxi, China, 2009

　　无锡市的伯渎港流淌着中国最古老的运河——伯渎河。伯渎河修建于史前，是一条见证了无锡3000多年历史并为无锡发展做出贡献的河流。伯渎河流域是我国物产丰厚的粮仓之一，以水运为基础，密切联系着人们的生活，在无锡拥有不可或缺的存在感。

　　近年，伴随着高度的城市开发以及工业化进程，人口急速增长，由于相应配套的污水处理等基础配套设施滞后，导致水质恶化，使生态平衡遭到破坏。

　　这次，在整备基础设施的同时，立案建造一个以运河为中心的全新都市。旨在将无锡市构建成理想水乡，把都市、人、自然三者有机地结合在一起；传承、宣扬优良传统文化的同时，创造出新生活和文化，从而实现丰富多彩的都市生活的目标。

　　近18km的运河总体规划，围绕下述规划理念展开进行。

　　•在历史文化层面，实现"吴文化格调与现代设计的融合"、"创建新无锡标志、营造伯渎港独有韵味"。

　　•在水与生态层面，实现"通过疏浚淤泥来改善水质以及生态环境"，"重新构建城市与自然的关联"。

　　•在观光与交通层面，"再建连接城市与自然的水上交通工程"，"通过整合生态脉对旅游业和经济活动产生巨大的促进作用"。

　　2010年9月，作为起点的"泰伯文化广场公园"工程已部分竣工。后期地块的城市规划将与之连动，运河公园与绿地规划也将依次推进。在不久的将来，公园竣工之际，希望其作为无锡市的标志，成为一个深受广大市民和游客喜爱的永久使用的空间。

The Bodu Port of Wuxi City is a valuable prehistoric canal that has contributed to the development of Wuxi for nearly three thousand years. The region being one of the major granaries in China, the shipping industry has been deeply rooted in people's daily lives.

Nevertheless, due to remarkable progress of the urban development and industrialization of recent years, the population has rapidly increased leaving the infrastructure such as sewage system lagging behind causing the water quality to deteriorate, stench, and aggravating the ecosystem.

This time, along with establishment of the infrastructure, a new urban planning centralizing around the canal was proposed. Aiming for a waterside utopia of Wuxi City; structuring an organic relation of the city and the people, respecting the history and its culture, and yet creating a new lifestyle and culture for an enriched urban life was objected.

A project for 15km of the canal was developed based on the following concepts:

- In respect of cultural history: "Fusion of Wu culture style and contemporary design, " and "Creation of a Bodu Port identity as a new symbol of Wuxi."

- In standpoint of water and ecology: "Improvements of water quality and ecological environment by dredging contaminated sediment," and "Restructuring the relationship of the city and nature."

- In standpoint of tourism and transportation: "Restructure water transportation to unify urbanity and nature," and "Synergistic effect of networking ecosystem for the tourist industry and economical activities."

Currently, as of November 2009, the base point of the project, the construction of Taibo Park is underway. Successively, along with the urban redevelopment project of the mountain area in the rear, a canal park and green tract constructions will proceed. We hope as the project completes in the near future, as a symbol of the city of Wuxi, it will become and endure as a place to be loved and enjoyed by the residents as well as tourists for many years.

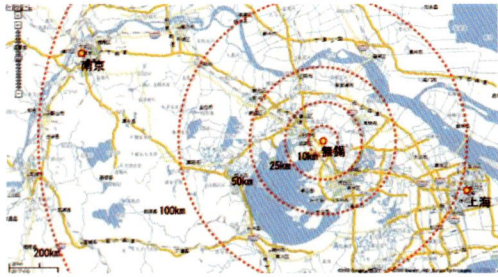

无锡市优良级旅游资源分布

三、绿化系统规划

规划范围内的公园用地总量为 11.86 公顷，街头绿地总量为 142.2 公顷，防护绿地总量为 8.72 公顷。

规划形成三个主要景观节点、四个次要景观节点。三个主要景观节点分别是泰伯广场、梅里古镇、梁鸿湿地，分别位于江溪、梅村、鸿山区段内，除此之外，另有吴地风华、滨水公园、革命公园、环鸿公园四个次要景观节点。

公园绿化以绿地为主，布置连续的步行通道，局部点缀少量休闲建筑及商业建筑，便于人们驻足停留，同时加强对植物配置的管理，形成富有地方特色的绿化空间。

规划不仅要解决功能与水质层面上的现存问题，更重要的是要持续、长久地保护伯渎河流域的生态和环境。随着无锡城市化进程的加快，人口的增长速度也将更加迅速，这势必会加大维护自然环境与生态系统的工作难度。正因如此，本次规划在解决当前功能与水质问题的基础上，更重视对伯渎河流域生态环境的可持续规划。

本规划不仅要将伯渎港作为改善环境、建设城区的范本，还要让伯渎河成为今后的新城市轴线。让其发展成为重新构建"城市"、"人"、"自然"关系的轴线。展示在未来的城市发展过程中人们对自然与生态应该持有的姿态。

3000 年历史的转折点
未来 3000 年的构想……

水乡理想都市——无锡

标志性轴线

新城市轴线——伯渎港

"城市"、"人"、"自然"的关系

重新审视、调整、构建"城市"、"人"、"自然"的关系（复兴博大精深的文化）

促进发展"城市"、"人"、"自然"的关系，寻求新视野与方向（引入新文化、协调新与旧）

摸索顺应时代与社会，具有弹性与灵活性的"城市"、"人"、"自然"（创造和摸索新文化）

创造出为时代添彩的文化

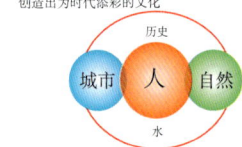

20 世纪型城市轴线

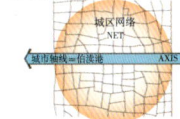

21 世纪 + 城市与生活共生轴线

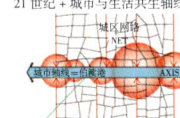

无锡是在伯渎港基础上发展起来的城市（NET）

沿构成城市骨架的轴线形成街区
发挥地形与地势优势的土地利用

功能与效率优先的社会加入无视地形与地势的城市轴线

城市与生活的关系缺位

构造、调和 20 世纪功能与效率优先的城市格局形成可持续发展的城市构造

通过重新构建和发展本应有的伯渎港创造出新的文化
重新构建与发展"城市"、"人"、"自然"的关系

伯渎港总体规划方针

景观转折点 -1
"衔接城市与近郊的节点"

景观转折点 -2
"衔接历史区域的节点（接近城市部分）"

景观转折点 -3
"衔接历史区域的节点（接近自然部分）"

景观转折点 -4
"衔接 20 世纪型城市轴线（调整公路）的节点"

景观转折点 -5
"衔接近郊住宅的节点"

城市

自然

① 新河道旗舰区域
• 连接现有主城区的节点
• 与 20 世纪型城市相协调、融合
• 成为今后城市建设范本的街区
• 新文化、信息的发源地

② 商住功能的城市型河岸生活
• 新旧住宅、商业设施之间的协调与融合
• 拥有河岸优势的商业设施及娱乐设施
• 设置高品质、雅致的设施
• 生活与观光相协调
• 提高人们生活意识水准

③ 水文化·学习区域
～水科学馆～
• 与水互动的各种体验空间
• 伯渎港的水质管理
• 城市型水质净化设施（水质净化工）
供应各种区域
• 参观工厂
• 介绍伯渎港的变迁及水的重要性

④ 感受吴的历史区域
• 以泰伯庙为中心，建设感受历史的街区
• 围绕泰伯、伯渎港建立吴的历史资源馆
• 开发以伯渎河孕育的农作物、水产品主题的商业
• 恢复和新增祭祀、庆典活动
• 配合上述活动运营、策划游览内容

⑤ 充满自然元素的近郊型河岸生活
• 提议建设富有稻田风情的生活区域
• 接近位于东部的原生态自然区域
▽ 观光据点
• 提供当地农产品与水产品的物产馆
• 新设江南水乡淡水水族馆

⑥ 感受江南水乡自然韵味的区域
• 充分感受江南水乡自然韵味的区域
• 观光农园（参与插秧、割稻，采摘葡萄、采菱、采莲等活动）
• 结合湿地公园设置观察、学习生态的场所（鸟类乐园、水的生物净化等）
• 与湿地公园内的历史博物馆融为一体的江南水乡风景

贯穿本规划的要点
〇将吴文化与江南水乡风情作为景观规划设计的着重点，运用于从城市到自然的所有区域。
例如：人行天桥、休息设施的设计等
〇通过这种手段表现人的参与，展现生活感，从而最大限度地描绘人与自然的关联性。

总体规划平面图（部分）

■a 剖面图比例 1：1000

河滨旗舰区规划（竞标方案）

娱乐设施

屋顶花园

店铺、餐馆

文化设施

花园广场

交流庭园

a 剖面图

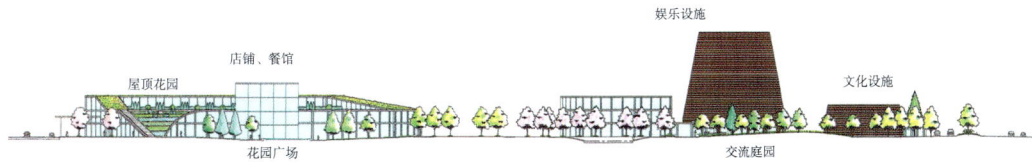

■b 剖面图比例 1：1000

水上巴士候船中心
信息馆
水岸眺望馆   栈桥（水上巴士登船处）

草坪广场

伯渎港

b 剖面图

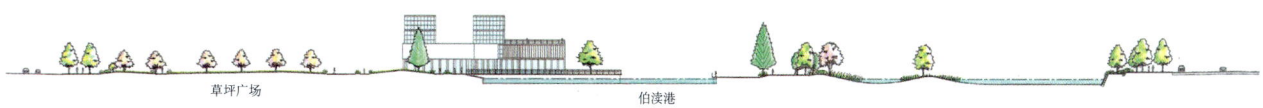

■c 断面图比例 1：1000

伯渎港

c 剖面图

泰伯文化广场夜景（竞标方案）

泰伯文化广场作为城市广场与商业设施形成一个整体（竞标方案）

设置提高广场象征性的水池和跌水小品

视线诱导设计增强了被道路分隔的广场的一体感

将来园者从新设道路引向伯渎港散步道

新设路桥的桥下小径

观望泰伯像和梅山的水边广场

从位于中央的泰伯大道到水边的空间

与泰伯文化广场形成一体感的泰伯大道人行道空间

河滨旗舰区的全景图（竞标方案）

位于道路交叉部的街角广场

建造街角标志

商业设施前的庭园空间

进入商业空间的人行道

宛如轻振翅羽的水鸟，又如同驻桨的小舟般优美的门户桥梁。

门户桥的夜景作为标志性建筑物，浮现在夜空的优美姿态。

拥有映照雕塑般身影的池面广场

以现代形式展现江南水乡岸边楼阁的水上餐厅

明快并具透明感的圆弧形水上回廊

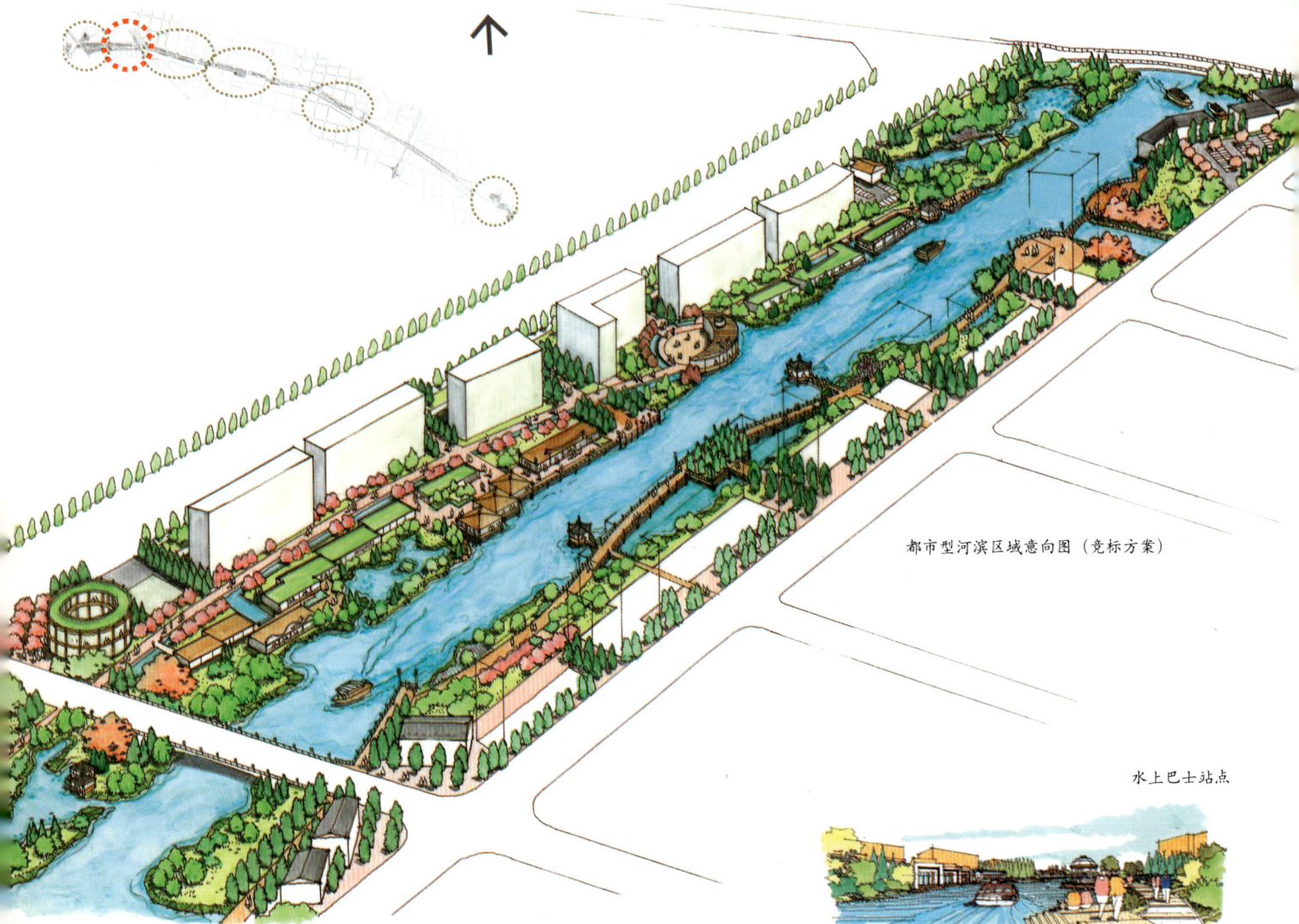

都市型河滨区域意向图（竞标方案）

水上巴士站点

将水引入后部商业设施

湿地公园的餐厅与大温室

湿地公园内的散步道

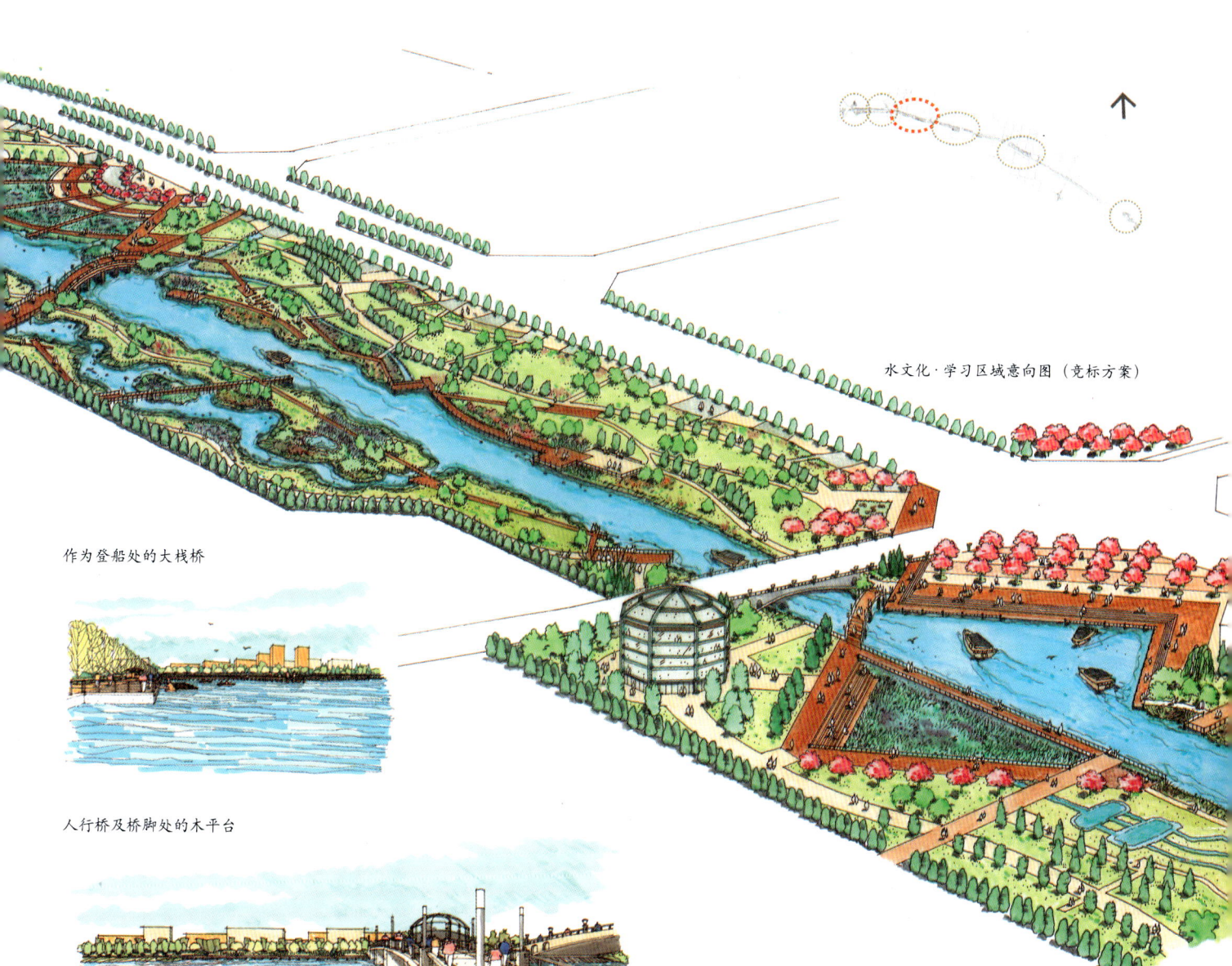

水文化·学习区域意向图（竞标方案）

作为登船处的大栈桥

人行桥及桥脚处的木平台

与路桥和人行桥相连的水边景观

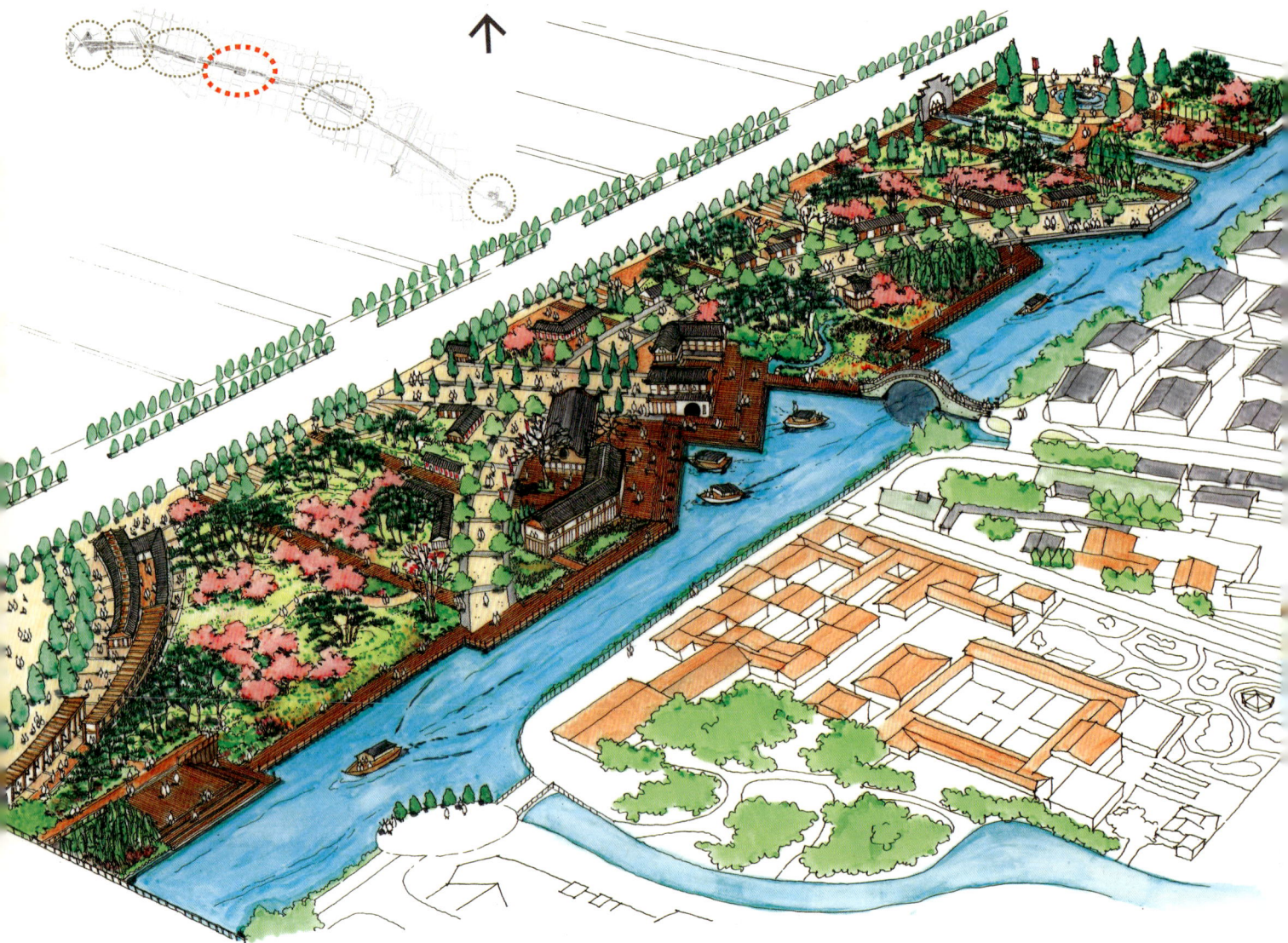

感受吴的历史区域意向图（竞标方案）

展现河川汇集点风采的列柱

通向商业设施的人行桥

融入传统建筑意向的商业设施

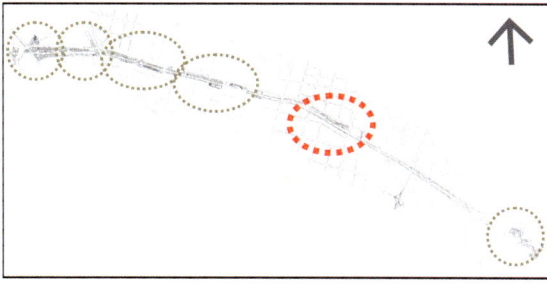

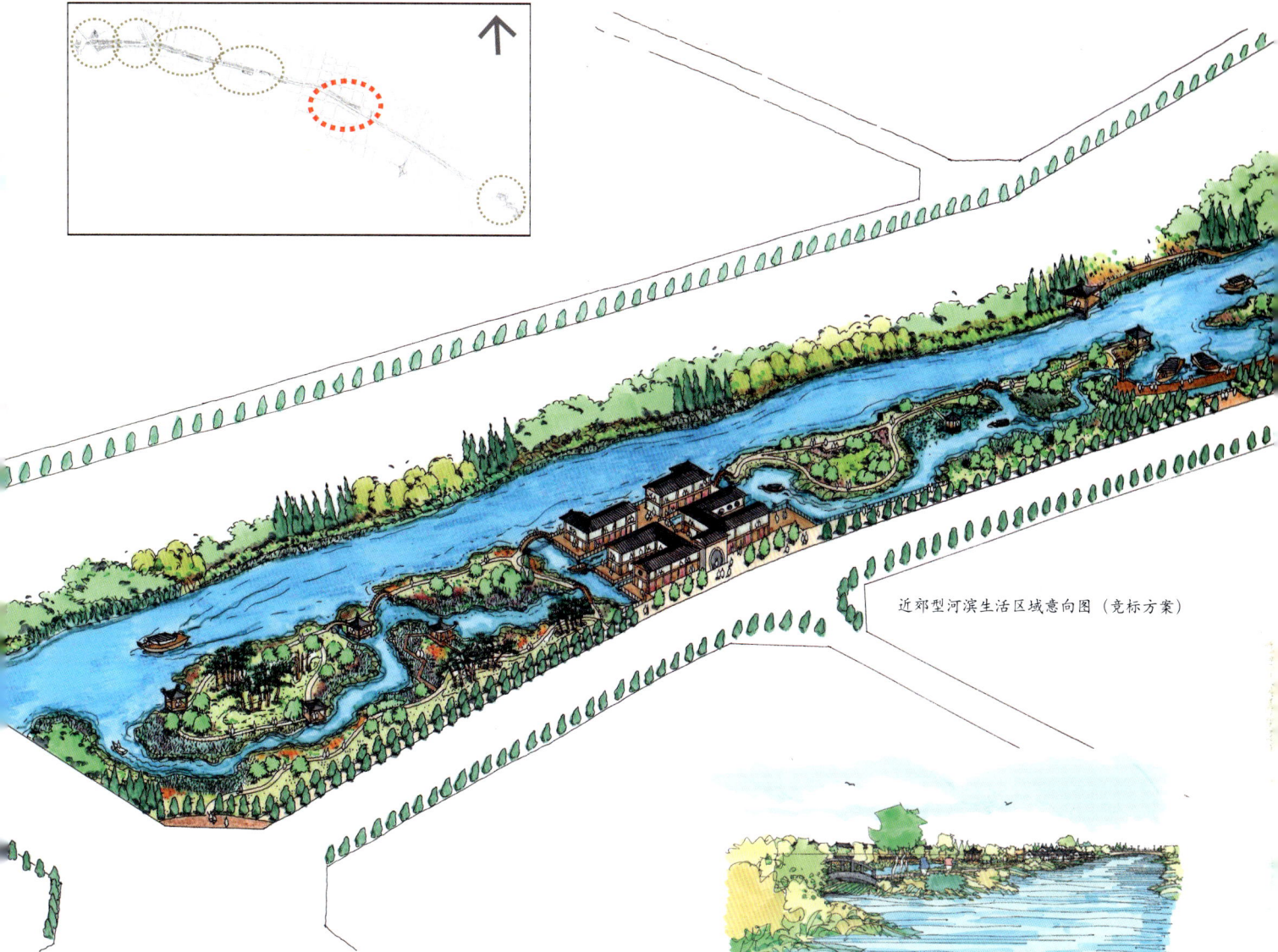

近郊型河滨生活区域意向图（竞标方案）

与商业设施相连的自然散步道

作为河川分叉处标志性建筑的江南水乡淡水水族馆

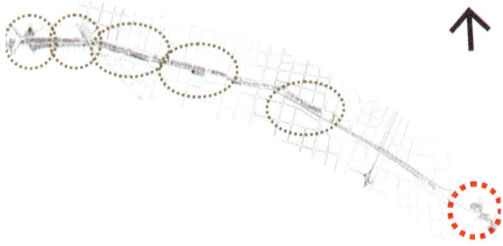

感受江南水乡区域意向图（竞标方案）

充分享受水乡风景的环游型道路

设施名称

A：公交候车站・停车场　　H：湿地植物观察地带
B：现有村庄　　　　　　　I：水鸟观察用房
C：住宿设施　　　　　　　J：稻田
D：野营地　　　　　　　　K：体验型制作工坊
E：野营地管理用房　　　　L：水上巴士登船处
F：访客中心
G：昆虫观察地带

生态观察区域意向图

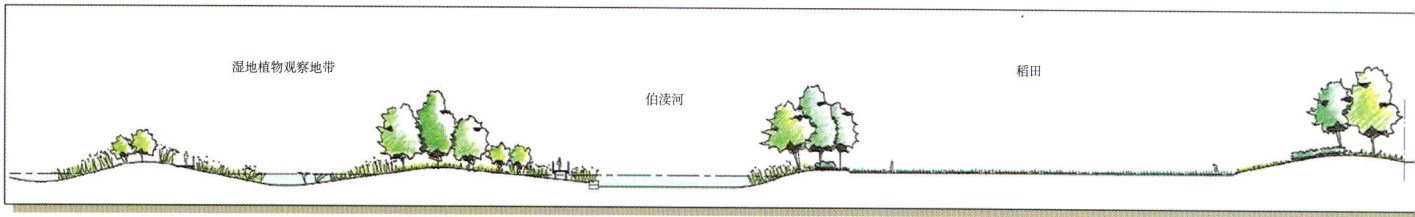

湿地植物观察地带　　　　　　　　　　　　　　　　　伯渎河　　　　　　　　　　　　　　　稻田

a 断面图

◇伯渎港画卷

　　本规划以伯渎河为中心轴，紧扣城市、自然、历史之间的关联性对景观进行规划设计。本规划更是重新构筑人与水之间密切关系的规划，为此在河岸设置了多种多样的景观。

　　本页是伯渎港画卷的一个缩影，展现了伯渎港未来的美景。

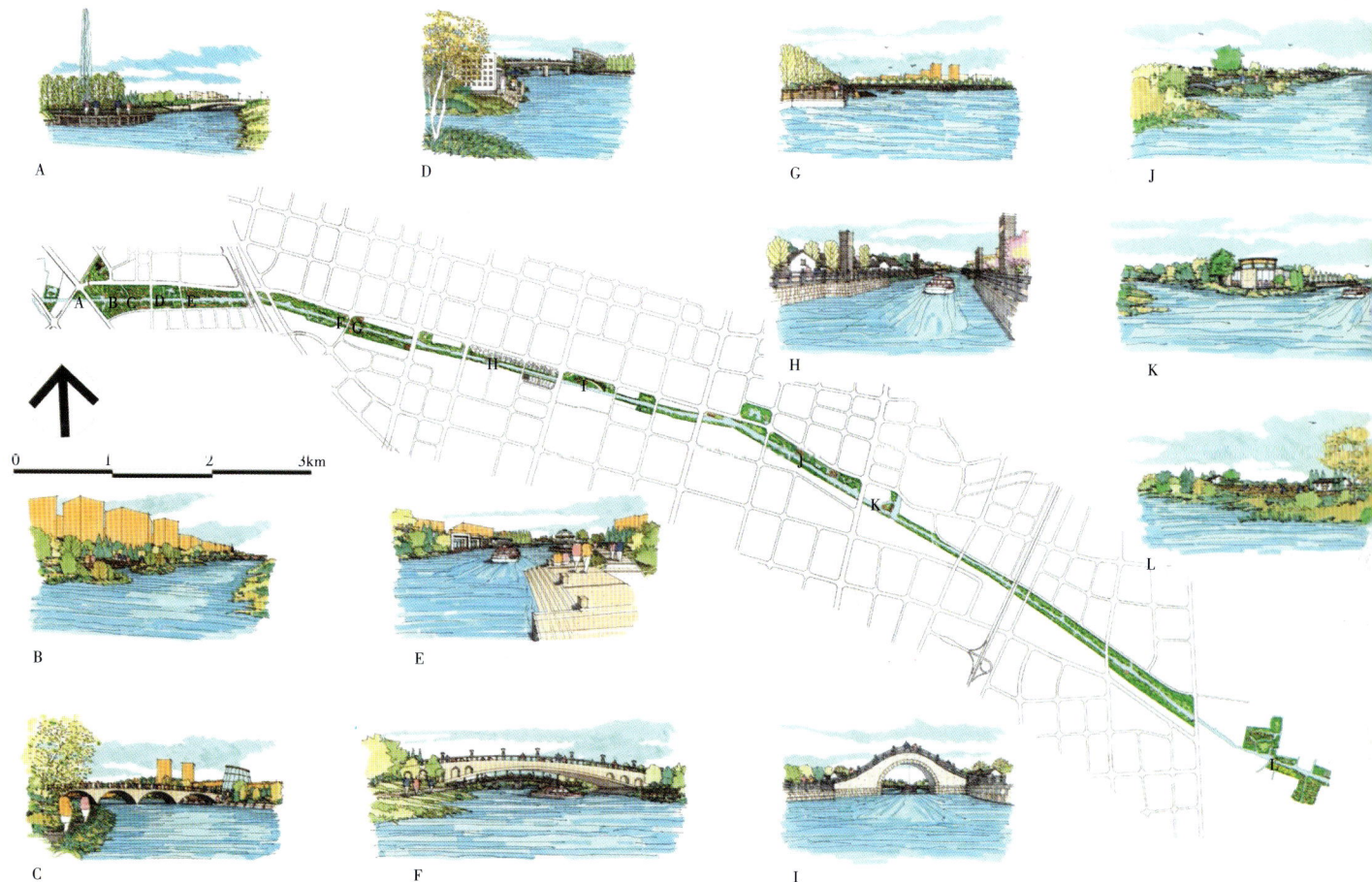

A

D

G

J

H

K

B

E

L

C

F

I

项目名称 ： 2005 年爱・地球博景观设计
地点 ： 爱知县长久町
业主 ： （财）2005 日本国际博览会协会
设计・监督 ： 户田芳树 须藤哲 大桥尚美 清水达也 吉泽 力 友部洋子
相关设施 ： 菊竹清训建筑设计事务所
施工 ： 日比谷 Amensu 集团，西武造园集团 等
设计时间 ： 2002 年 1 月～2005 年 3 月
施工时间 ： 2003 年 4 月～2005 年 3 月
规模 ： 158 hm²
主要设施 ： 日本广场、大花坛、爱・地球博广场、空中木栈道、各大门、各组团
摄影 ： 户田芳树 大桥尚美

项目名称 ： 群马县立"群马昆虫之林"景观设计
地点 ： 群马县桐生市新里町
业主 ： 群马县政府
设计・监督 ： 方案规划：户田芳树 须藤哲 小河原孝生（生态计划研究所）
方案设计：户田芳树 须藤哲 大桥幸雄
施工图设计：须藤哲 大桥幸雄 古贺健一
相关设施 ： 昆虫观察馆 （株）安藤忠雄建筑研究所
施工 ： 中部总合开发（有限公司）等
设计时间 ： 1996 年 8 月～2005 年 3 月
施工时间 ： 1999 年 11 月～2005 年 8 月
规模 ： 48 hm²
主要设施 ： 杂木林、观察小道、桑田果树园、原生态区、体验工作室等
摄影 ： 户田芳树

项目名称 ： 羽生农林公园景观设计
地点 ： 埼玉县羽生市三田谷
业主 ： 羽生市政府
设计・监督 ： 方案规划：（株）北山创造研究所、（株）K 计划事务所
方案・施工图设计：户田芳树 须藤哲 大桥幸夫
相关设施 ： 北山孝二郎（株）K 计划事务所
施工 ：
设计时间 ： 1999 年 7 月～2000 年 8 月
施工时间 ： 1999 年 12 月～2001 年 3 月
规模 ： 3.6 hm²
主要设施 ： 标志惶景观山丘、景观池、流水、调整池、生态观察区域 亲水平台、人行桥、车行桥等
摄影 ： 户田芳树

项目名称 ： 向岛洋兰中心景观设计
地点 ： 广岛县尾道市向岛町
业主 ： 尾道市政府
设计・监督 ： 户田芳督 须藤哲 清水达也
相关设施 ： 建筑监督 冈河贡 设计（株）泉创建 Engineering
施工 ： （有）吉原造园 等
设计时间 ： 1993 年 9 月～1994 年 3 月
施工时间 ： 1994 年 4 月～1995 年 4 月
规模 ： 3.4 hm²
主要设施 ： 涌水池、流水、池塘、圆形道路、桥、绿地广场、休息广场
摄影 ： 户田芳树

项目名称 ： 仙寿庵前庭
地点 ： 群马县利根郡水上町
业主 ： 谷川旅馆
设计・监督 ： 户田芳树
相关设施 ： 无
施工 ： 大利根造园土木（株）
设计时间 ： 2003 年 10 月～2004 年 3 月
施工时间 ： 2004 年 4 月～7 月
规模 ： 2000 m²
主要设施 ： 瀑布、流水、池塘、天然石材铺装、庭院假山、龙安寺墙、入口大门（仿桂离宫）
摄影 ： 户田芳树

项目名称 ： 梦之岛热带温室景观设计
地点 ： 东京都江东区梦之岛
业主 ： 东京都政府
设计・监督 ： 户田芳树 木福由纪 倒川清史 伊藤直博
相关设施 ： 建筑 大字根・江平建筑事务所
施工 ： （株）石胜外景设计 等
设计时间 ： 1985 年 4 月～1986 年 3 月
施工时间 ： 1986 年 7 月～1987 年 10 月
规模 ： 占地面积 24.7hm² 建筑面积 3900 m²
主要设施 ： 大瀑布、流水、池塘、隧道、凉亭、桥、热带植物
摄影 ： 伊藤直博

项目名称 ： 道路驿站"天童温泉"
地点 ： 山形县天童市贵津锹之町
业主 ： 天童市政府
设计・监督 ： 户田芳树 清水达也 友部洋子
相关设施 ： 森林信息馆、特产馆、八音盒博物馆
施工 ： 东海林建设（株）
设计时间 ： 1999 年 6 月～2003 年 8 月
施工时间 ： 2000 年 9 月～2004 年 3 月
规模 ： 6 hm²
主要设施 ： 多功能广场、草坪广场、露天舞台、厕所、喷水、音乐游乐设施 多功能灯光照明、象棋雕塑小品
摄影 ： 泷浦秀雄

项目名称 ： 大沼一丁目公园
地点 ： 日本 东京都 小平市
业主 ： 东京都政府
设计・监督 ： 清水达也、友部洋子、石井博史
设计时间 ： 2000 年 06 月～2000 年 10 月
施工时间 ： 2000 年 11 月～2001 年 03 月
规模 ： 5800 m²
主要设施 ： 草坪广场、水池、水流、花架、儿童游乐器材
摄影 ： 户田芳树

项目名称 ： 真光寺公园景观设计
地点 ： 东京都町田市真光寺町
业主 ： 都市再生机构东日本分部
设计・监督 ： 方案规划：户田芳树 奈木造率
方案・施工图设计：户田芳树 清水达也
相关设施 ： 无
施工 ： 芝茂造园建设（株）等
设计时间 ： 1995 年 7 月～1996 年 10 月
施工时间 ： 1995 年 10 月～1997 年 3 月
规模 ： 3.8 hm²
主要设施 ： 草地、景观池、门户雕塑小品、4 个凉亭、管理用楼、厕所、木栈道、游乐设施、停车场
摄影 ： 户田芳树

项目名称	：中京大学农田校园景观设计
地点	：爱知县丰田市贝津町
业主	：学校法人 梅村学园中京大学
设计·监督	：户田芳树 吉泽力
相关设施	：创意栏 小峰贵芳
施工	：（株）石田组、三井住友建设（株）
设计时间	：2003 年 1 月～2006 年 12 月
施工时间	：2004 年 4 月～2007 年 5 月
规模	：4.2 hm²
主要设施	：丘陵区域的圆形池塘、雕塑小品、中心广场、榉树散步道、原生态区域的流水与池塘、栈道、枕木广场、休息广场
摄影	：户田芳树

项目名称	：尾道市立大学校园景观设计
地点	：广岛县尾道市久山町
业主	：尾道市立大学
设计·监督	：户田芳树 清水达也 山崎真理 友部洋子
相关设施	：无
施工	：（株）大宝组
设计时间	：1993 月 9 月～1995 年 12 月
施工时间	：1994 年 1 月～1996 年 5 月
规模	：3000 m²
主要设施	：雕塑小品、栈道、凉亭、景观墙、铁板景墙、树池式坐凳
摄影	：户田芳树

项目名称	：大连医科学院
地点	：中国 大连市
业主	：大连医科学院
设计·监督	：户田芳树、吉泽力
设计时间	：2004 年 3 月～2006 年 11 月
施工时间	：2006 年 12 月～2007 年 10 月
规模	：110 hm²
主要设施	：纪念广场、中央广场、海之广场、海滨广场、休憩之丘、象征之丘、气息之丘
摄影	：户田芳树

项目名称	：一之江名人老屋景观设计地点
地点	：东京都江户川区春江町
业主	：田岛铆子（房屋所有人）
设计·监督	：户田芳树 大桥尚美 友部洋子
相关设施	：无
施工	：小池农园 等
设计时间	：1998 年 6 月～1999 年 4 月
施工时间	：1998 年 10 月～1999 年 4 月
规模	：6394 m²
主要设施	：建筑物（长屋门、房屋、仓库）、前庭、中庭、主庭、庭园树林、耕地遗迹、外护城河、内护城河
摄影	：户田芳树

项目名称	：本乡富士山公园景观设计
地点	：神奈川县横滨市荣区中野町
业主	：横滨市
设计·监督	：方案设计：户田芳树 吉泽力 山内润子
	施工图设计：大桥尚美 吉泽力 山内润子 金井幸雄 友部洋子
	设计监督：吉泽力
相关设施	：小岩井家的搬迁古代民居施工
施工	：生驹造园（株） 口町造园（株）等
设计时间	：1998 年 5 月～2002 年 3 月
施工时间	：2000 年 4 月～2003 年 3 月
规模	：10 hm²
主要设施	：长屋门、古式民居、工作室用楼、厕所、耕地、烧炭场、梅林等
摄影	：户田芳树

项目名称	：森柏龙宫殿日本庭院
地点	：奥地利森柏龙宫殿
业主	：奥地利政府
	规划构思 原田荣进（日本园林协会）
设计·监督	：户田芳树
相关设施	：休闲茶楼、入口大门
施工	：小口基实（小口庭院 Green Exterior）岸本平晃（岸本驹造园）等
设计时间	：1907 年 1 月～1998 年 2 月
施工时间	：1998 年 5 月～1998 年 11 月
规模	：1200 m²
主要设施	：用当地天然石堆砌的假山、铺装石、踏脚石、原产日本的材料建造的建仁寺墙、竹编篱笆、金阁寺墙、光悦寺墙、洗手钵、灯笼、水琴窟、茶室入口处的"鹿吓"

项目名称	：无锡新区泰伯文化广场
地点	：中国 无锡市
业主	：无锡新区经济发展集团总公司
设计·监督	：户田芳树、吉泽力、古贺健一
设计时间	：2009 年 1 月～2009 年 5 月
施工时间	：2009 年 6 月～2010 年 1 月
规模	：8 hm²
主要设施	：水边餐厅、泰伯像、景观小品、河溪、草坪广场、亲水护岸

公司概要

Company Profile

株式会社　户田芳树风景计画　Yoshiki Toda Landscape & Architects

Address	151-0053	3F Miyuki BLDG
	东京都涩谷区代々木 1-36-1 ミユキビル 3F	1-36-1 Yoyogi Shibuya-ku Tokyo 151-0053 Japan
Tel	+81-3-3320-8601	
Fax	+81-3-3320-8610	
E-Mail	info @ todafu.co.jp	
Homepage	http://www.todafu.co.jp	

户田芳树　Yoshiki TODA　董事长

履历 ： 1970 年东京农业大学农学部造园学科毕业
1981 年绿色津南中央广场
1984 年诹访湖畔公园
1986 年梦之岛公园—热带植物馆
1998 年森柏龙宫殿日本庭园
2005 年爱 · 地球世界博览会景观总监
2009 年无锡市泰伯公园
研究课题 ： 日本文化和庭园的关系与其形式
资格 ： 注册景观设计师 (RLA)
一级造园施工管理技师

大桥尚美　Naomi OHASHI　董事

履历 ： 1975 年千叶大学木材工艺科毕业
2003 年 Master Garden 住宅
2005 年爱 · 地球世界博览会会场绿化 · 修景规划
2006 年江户川区厅广场的修景
2006 年宇城市誉之丘 · 荻尾溜池周边
2007 年高知县五台山花道的道路整修计划
2008 年滨松植物造型世界博览会会场修景规划
研究课题 ： 关于在景观空间中花的修景技巧
资格 ： 注册景观设计师 (RLA)
一级造园施工管理技师
二级土木施工管理技师
公园管理运营师

吉泽　力　Tsutomu YOSHIZAWA　董事

履历 ： 1983 年东京农业大学农学部造园学科毕业
2004 年爱 · 地球世界博览会钟塔
2005 年丰洲站前地区一类市区改造工程的景观
2006 年沈阳长白万科城景观
2007 年中京大学丰田校园景观
2007 年大连医科大学校园景观
2008 年北京龙湖唐宁 ONE 项目
研究课题 ： 运用大地造型展开对空间的设计，同时配以细致的造园技术创造
资格 ： 注册景观设计师 (RLA)
一级造园施工管理技师
一级土木施工管理技师

大桥幸雄　Yukio OHASHI　董事

履历 ： 1994 年多摩美术大学美术学部 2 部设计学科毕业
2000 年羽生农林公园
2001 年热海梅园韩国庭园
2002 年群马昆虫森林
2007 年沈阳佳和欧洲新城
研究课题 ： 景观造型物体和植物所带来的心理效果
资格 ： 注册景观设计师 (RLA)
一级造园施工管理技师
二级造园技师

清水达也　Tatsuya SHIMIZU　主设计师

履历 ： 1985 年武藏野美术大学造型部建筑学科毕业
2001 年 UR 西晋与环境和谐共处型住宅
2002 年丰洲 3 丁目公园
2003 年爱·地球世界博览会会场绿化·修景规划
2004 年道路驿站"天童温泉"
2006 年狭山市车站西口地区市区改造造园工程
2007 年羽田空港国际机候楼景观
研究课题 ： 谕之为"日本的空间"的近代景观设计
资格 ： 注册景观设计师 (RLA)
一级造园施工管理技师
一级建筑师

古贺健一　Kenichi KOGA　主设计师

履历 ： 1996 年九州艺术工科大学研究生学院生活环境专业毕业
2000 年新川丸池公园
2004 年 Verdeal 市川南
2007 年蒲郡站前广场
2008 年茅崎城址公园
研究课题 ： 营建轻松、愉悦的空间
资格 ： 注册景观设计师 (RLA)
一级造园施工管理技师

石井博史　Hiroshi ISHII　主设计师

履历 ： 1998 年东京农业大学造园学科毕业
2005 年热海市梅园
2006 年狭山市车站西口地区市区改造造园工程
2007 年 Gardenier 钻景观
2008 年 Viequ Stage 北千住景观
研究课题 ： 关于住宅空间的景观设计手法
资格 ： 注册景观设计师 (RLA)
一级造园施工管理技师

高冲　哉　Hajime TAKAOKI　设计师

履历 ： 2003 年千叶大学研究生院自然科学研究学科结业
2004 年丰洲地区 8–2 街区设计方针
2005 年丰洲 3 丁目住宅景观
2007 年羽田机场国际航线候机楼景观
研究课题 ： 对山谷地区幻灯片式连续景观的评价与研究
资格 ： 注册景观设计师 (RLA)

堀井大辅　Daisuke HORII　设计师

履历 ： 2006 年东京农业大学研究生院农学研究科造园学专业结业
2007 年江户川区百合木公园
2008 年旧伊藤博文别邸外围景观
2008 年冲绳宜野湾第一街区景观
2009 年入会的整修工程景观
一级造园施工管理技师

平田惠理　Eri HIRATA

坂本光得　Mitsunori SAKAMOTO

池田　葵　Aoi IKEDA

岩田かおり　Kaori IWATA

半洋　薫　Kaoru IINAGAWA

须藤　哲　Satoru SUTOH

中国

刘佳　中国代表

履历 ： 2003 年神户商科大学毕业
2008 年北京龙湖唐宁 ONE
2009 年无锡新区伯渎港河道景观
2010 年苏州仁恒塘北小区
2010 年重庆瑞安龙华桥住宅

林振铭　设计师

履历 ： 2000 年日本东京农业大学造园学士毕业
2002 年日本东京农业大学造园硕士毕业
2006 年沈阳长白万科城景观
2006 年沈阳花博会盘锦园、抚顺园景观设计
2007 年大连医科大学校园景观
2007 年沈阳佳和欧洲新城

编后语　Afterword

公司自成立以来，一晃便 30 年。我于 20 世纪 70 年代大学毕业，正逢日本经济高度发展的鼎盛期；1980 年代创立公司的时候，经济成长的盛势尤在。我承接了来自国家、地方政府和私营企业的许多项目，留下了为数不少的作品。能生逢这样的时代真是值得庆幸。

值得回味的作品很多，其中有些在历经 20 多年后，出现了一些我没想到的变化，我也时常会为一些未曾预见到的使用功能而惊叹。景观设计中大量地运用自然素材，树木成长之后，会展现超出设计意图的规模与气势，让我感受自然的力量，于是便坦然地接受了这个超出设计意图的空间了。换句话说，景观设计作为一个契机，为空间赋予新的物语，我感受到了这一点，于是，也欣然接受了这个新的物语空间。愿风景在悠然的时间长河中永存……

这是我在中国出版的第二本书。非常感谢中国给予我这样的机会，同时也非常感谢以下人士所给予的支持与帮助。

撰写本书卷首语的俞孔坚教授、章俊华教授；日翻英的寺崎直子和日翻中的刘佳，以及提供帮助的董犇、陆凌雁和梅慧敏老师，感谢他们把难以理解的日文编译成朗朗上口的英文和中文；中国建筑工业出版社第三图书中心的白玉美主任和戚琳琳编辑，感谢她们给予的建议；提供本书照片、图纸以及排版的全体工作人员，感谢他们的辛勤工作。

户田芳树
2010 年 10 月

译者后记　Translator's Afterword

可以说这本书倾注了户田事务所全体员工，特别是户田老师诸多的心血。从策划到出版，历时将近两年半。为了奉上最新的项目资料，户田老师利用休息时间亲自到现场拍照、亲自甄选出版照片。无论是真情流露的"我与景观"，还是每个项目的设计说明，户田老师都是几经考虑之后才落笔成文的。这是一本有关风景的书，也是一本记录景观设计师心路历程和成长足迹的书。无论是刚毕业的学生，还是资深的景观设计者，相信用心的读者一定会从书中找寻到属于自己的那份感悟与收获。

对学管理出身的我而言，能有幸主笔翻译本书，算得上是生命中的一段传奇。非常感谢户田事务所全体员工对我的支持和信任。作为一名非专业人士，对于户田事务所作品的理解更多地停留在图片与文字上，在此将一些体会记录下来，与读者共享，希望大家能从不同的角度了解户田事务所的作品。

文章的字里行间，首先让我感受到的是"真诚"。

在每个作品的最后，都有一段类似总结的感想，从中读者可以认知到作品对于设计者的教诲。正因为户田事务所的员工拥有真诚对待设计项目的心态、真诚学习与吸收项目自身所具备的优势与潜质、真诚处理每一次与自然接触的机会，所以他们可以从每一次的设计中得到超出设计之外的感悟。

与场地如水乳交融般的设计。

老子曾说过"上善若水。水善利万物而不争……"。户田事务所的作品具有这样的特质。每一篇的设计都如水一般，汇入周边的环境，相互浸润，你中有我、我中有你，如天成般自然，无娇柔做作之感。所有的设计与那片土地是一种对话的关系，竭尽全力地展现土地所拥有的内涵与魅力，丝毫不会有凌驾于场地之上的态度。

运筹帷幄于胸的气概。

所有作品的动线和周边景观的连接都非常流畅，如一气呵成般。这便是功底，需要拥有承载整个环境的胸怀作基础。这也是持之以恒不断挖掘、不断追寻的结果。是一种坚持的同时，也是一种摒弃。坚持的是自己的风格以及对待每一个设计的态度，摒弃的是附庸和无法理会的要求。正是这种源于心灵的感受，为每一个作品赋予了灵魂。

整个翻译过程是艰辛的，户田事务所的员工不仅需要非常清晰地向我描绘文章中出现的场面，对一些专业词汇，还必须以通俗易懂的方式解释它们的含义。整个翻译过程让我再次感受到户田事务所员工对待工作的态度，他们始终秉着一成不变的认真与执着，做好手上的每一件事。他们总是以设计自己人生似的态度，对待所承接的每一个项目、所承诺的每一份工作。

希望读者对我稚嫩的翻译给予指导和批评，同时希望为更多的人架起与户田事务所沟通的桥梁，请将意见与感想发送至：todafu2010@163.com

刘佳
2010 年 11 月